COMING OUT TO PLAY

COMING OUT TO PLAY

ROBBIE ROGERS
with ERIC MARCUS

PENGUIN BOOKS

PENGUIN BOOKS

Published by the Penguin Group
Penguin Group (USA) LLC
375 Hudson Street
New York, New York 10014

USA | Canada | UK | Ireland | Australia | New Zealand | India | South Africa | China
penguin.com
A Penguin Random House Company
First published in Penguin Books 2014

"Leeds, Leeds, Leeds (Marching On Together)"
Published by Barry Mason Music, administration by Copyright Administration Services Ltd.
Words and music by Barry Mason and Les Reed; copyright © 1972 R.A.M. Music Ltd. and
Barry Mason Music Ltd.; copyright renewed.
All rights for R.A.M. Music Ltd. in the U.S. and Canada administered by Universal – Polygram
International Publishing, Inc.
All rights reserved. Used by permission.
Reprinted by permission of Hal Leonard Corporation

Photograph credits
Insert 1, page 1 (top and bottom), 3 (bottom), 4 (top), 5 (bottom), 6 (top),
    7 (top and bottom), 8 (top and bottom), insert 2, page 3 (bottom): Courtesy of
    Theresa Rarick Rogers
Page 2 (top and bottom), 3 (top), 4 (bottom), 5 (top), 6 (bottom): Courtesy of
    Robert H. Rogers Jr.
Insert 2, page 1 (top): Charlotte Observer / McClatchy-Tribune / Getty Images
Page 1 (bottom), 4 (bottom): Jeff Gross / Getty images Sport
Page 2 (top): Stephen Dunn / Getty Images Sport
Page 2 (bottom): Drew Hallowell / Getty Images Sport
Page 3 (top): Jamie Sabau / Getty Images Sport
Page 4 (top): Tom Jenkins / Getty Images Sport
Page 5, 7 (top): Courtesy of the author
Page 6: Danielle Levitt / August
Page 7 (middle): Victor Decolongon / Getty Images Sport
Page 7 (bottom): Jason Merritt / Getty Images Entertainment
Page 8: Carlos Serrao

LIBRARY OF CONGRESS CATALOGING-IN-PUBLICATION DATA
Rogers, Robbie.
Coming out to play / Robbie Rogers with Eric Marcus.
     pages cm
ISBN 978-0-14-312661-4
1. Rogers, Robbie.   2. Soccer players—United States—Biography.   3. Gay athletes—United
States—Biography.   I. Marcus, Eric.   II. Title.
GV942.7.R623A3 2014
796.334092—dc23
[B]

Printed in the United States of America
10 9 8 7 6 5 4 3 2 1

Set in Garth Graphic · Designed by Sabrina Bowers

For my family,
with so much love and appreciation

CONTENTS

ACKNOWLEDGMENTS

Although this book is a very personal effort, it required the help of many great people to make it all possible. First and foremost I would like to thank my family, including my beloved mother, Theresa Rarick Rogers; my devoted father, Robert H. Rogers, Jr.; my dear sisters, Alicia, Nicole, and Katie; and my loyal little brother (and favorite childhood playmate), Tim, for their love and support, and for opening up and sharing their personal stories.

Many thanks to my editor at Penguin Books, Patrick Nolan; Maxwell Reid, Patrick's assistant; and Steve Ross, my agent, for taking such good care of this project from beginning to end and for making everything run so smoothly. (Thank you, Max, for coordinating all the photographs!) Special thank-yous to Nick Misani, who designed the book's beautiful cover, to Lavina Lee, my eagle-eyed production editor, and to Bronwen Pardes, for masterfully transcribing the many hours of recorded interviews despite the fact that I talk so fast it's sometimes hard for my own family to understand me.

Debra Ware, Business and Community Liaison Director for the Leeds United Football Club in the UK, went above and beyond to welcome my coauthor to Leeds and provide an open door to Leeds United facilities and staff. I will also be forever indebted to Will Martin at the Just Grand! Vintage Tearoom in Leeds, for coming up with the perfect title, *Coming Out to Play*.

Finally, I am beyond grateful to Greg Berlanti, for inspiring me in so many ways. And, last, thank you to Eric Marcus, for being such an amazing cowriter and becoming such a good friend over the course of working together on this book.

INTRODUCTION

My name is Robbie Rogers. My sister Alicia calls me "Robber," but only when she's being affectionate and wants to make me smile. Mom calls me "Robbie" or "Dearheart" and a lot of other embarrassing things. Grammers and Grandpa call me "Obbie Ogers," not because they have a problem with their *r*'s but because *I* used to and they still like to think of me as their little grandson even though I long ago made peace with the entire alphabet. Most everyone else calls me Robbie.

Until recently I was best known as a professional soccer player who dabbled in fashion. (I have a men's clothing line.) I've played soccer in one form or another for twenty-two of my twenty-six years and during that time I've done what I've had to in order to fit in and excel in the game I love.

My fans know that I played for the Columbus Crew in Ohio for five seasons, was voted All-Star, and was named to the MLS Best XI, one of the biggest honors for a player in Major League Soccer, when we won the 2008 MLS Cup. They also know that

I played for the U.S. Olympic soccer team in the 2008 Beijing Summer Olympics (one of the highlights of my life), that I left the United States in 2012 to play "football" in England for Leeds United, and in May 2013 joined the LA Galaxy.

What I'm best known for now is having "blazed a trail," as NBA player Jason Collins said, when I returned to soccer after a very brief retirement and became the first openly gay male athlete to play in one of the top five team sports in North America.

Those are the bare outlines of my life. And while the various media have filled in some of the details since I came out publicly in February 2013, I've been uncomfortable with the shorthand versions of my life that I've seen and read. So in the pages that follow I'll tell you the story of my life behind the headlines, how I lived with a secret that just about destroyed me, how I came to free myself from that secret, and how, despite all my fears to the contrary, I found the kind of acceptance, support, and love that I never believed was possible.

My hope is that by reading the story of my life in greater depth you will learn something from my experience. While I wouldn't change anything about my life as I've lived it—because I wouldn't be where I am today if not for all the experiences I've had, both good and bad—I wish I'd known the high price you inevitably pay when you choose to keep a secret that compels you to live a lie.

It's a cliché to say that the truth will set you free. But as you'll see, that's exactly what happened to me. And it's that wish to live an open and honest life that inspires me now to share my story with you.

ROBBIE ROGERS
FEBRUARY 2014

COMING OUT TO PLAY

CHAPTER 1

CRACK-UP

I was out cold before my face hit the ground.

February 18, 2012, *should* have been one of the happiest days of my life. Instead, I was crumpled in a heap on the stunningly green pitch (what they call a sports field in England), unconsciously breathing in the scent of freshly cut grass.

If I'd been able to hear anything—and I guarantee you that I wasn't hearing a thing because my brain was still seeing stars—I could have heard a pin drop, because the twenty-one thousand soccer fans in the stands that sunny afternoon were holding their breath to see if the motionless American, who'd just made his debut at the historic Elland Road soccer stadium with their beloved Leeds United, was dead or alive.

Just the day before, I was as conscious as I'd ever been when I saw my name posted on the game-day roster at our training grounds for a match against the Doncaster Rovers. I can't say I

1

was surprised to see my name as much as I was relieved to finally have the chance to play after a month of training with my new team. Being placed on the game-day roster was no guarantee that I'd actually get to play, because I wasn't in the starting eleven (the eleven "footballers" who are designated to start the game). But if you don't get on the bench in the first place, there's no chance you'll be called in as a substitute.

It turned out to be a very dirty, ugly game—not much possession, not great passing—but even so, I enjoyed watching and just being there. The Leeds fans are very passionate. From the start of the game they're always chanting, singing, and cheering for their team.

Going into the second half the score was 0–0. There were five of us on the bench, and once the second half started the coach sent us to warm up at the side of the field, first two of us and then the other three. For a few minutes we jogged and stretched to get ready to possibly go in, and then went back to sit on the bench. And then I got called in.

You don't have a lot of time between getting called and the start of play, but in the few seconds it took to get from the bench to my position on the pitch I thought, *This is Leeds United. This is Elland Road. I'm playing football in England. I'm so proud and excited just being on this field where there's so much history and so many great footballers have played.*

Since I was a little boy kicking a ball up the steep driveway of the house where I grew up in Southern California, I'd dreamed of playing professional soccer in England. They have the biggest leagues and the most devoted fans, the game is always fast and competitive, and the greatest players want to go there. And now, having worked so hard to make this dream

2

come true, I was running onto the pitch for an English team for the first time. If I was at all nervous in that moment it was only because I was making my debut and was eager to make a great first impression with the fans. I had no idea just how big an impression I'd make.

I was only in the game for eleven minutes when one of our defenders kicked the ball up in the air. As it was coming down I challenged for the ball in hopes of winning possession for our team. I could see I was in a good position to head it toward our striker or the opposing team's goal. So I was backpedaling fast, thinking that I could connect with the ball and flick it off the back of my head. And at the same time, one of their defenders was racing flat-out from the opposite direction so he could flick the ball off the front of *his* head toward *our* goal. We both launched ourselves off the ground to meet the ball, but instead of connecting with the ball, my opponent head-butted me straight in the back of my head with the front of his—I was knocked out midair.

If anyone had known the real Robbie Rogers—and up to that point I'd made sure that no one did—they might have said it would take a blow to my head to get me to face facts about my life. But as I lay paralyzed on the field, fighting my way back to consciousness, all I could think was, *Where am I and how did I get here?* Good questions to consider in that brain-numbing moment—facedown in the grass, an ocean and a continent away from home.

CHAPTER 2

MY TWIN

I was a twin. I don't know how I sensed it without anyone ever telling me, but one day when I was six or seven years old I asked my mother if I'd had a twin brother. But instead of telling you what my mom told me happened to my twin, I thought I'd let her tell the story because she was there:

> We lived in San Pedro (which is part of Los Angeles) on Seventh Street in a little Spanish-style house right down the street from my office, where I had a legal practice. I was in the middle of a trial, but for some reason I needed to go to the house and either I'd forgotten my key or the key didn't work. There was a side window that I'd always left open a crack, so I decided to climb in, not even thinking that it was a foolish thing to do considering that I was three months pregnant. The window was maybe four feet

5

off the ground and I'm only five feet tall, so it was a bit of a struggle to get up to the window, and I slipped and fell.

It wasn't until I had some spotting and bleeding later that day that I realized there might be a problem. So I called my doctor, John Roller, who was a dear friend. In fact, he'd delivered two of my mother's children. He said, "You need to come in right now." And I said, "I'm in trial, but I'll come in after court today." Sometimes I think about my behavior at that time and wonder, *Was I nuts to wait?* But I waited and once he examined me he told me I was having a miscarriage and that he wanted me to go to the hospital for a D&C (dilation and curettage, which is a procedure to remove any remaining tissue from the pregnancy). I said, "No, I can't, I'm in trial." As you might imagine, I was extremely upset and was probably in denial about what was happening to me and by focusing on the trial I didn't have to think about losing my baby.

So the doctor said, "I'm going to give you a prescription that will at least slough off the majority of the lining of your uterus, and I want you to promise me you'll get it and take this medication tonight." I promised I would and I did. I don't know how I managed in the days and weeks that followed, because I had just lost this child and went through a postpartum depression of sorts, but I dealt with the trial, and looked after my two young daughters, and kept going.

Approximately four months after this miscarriage, I was still feeling like I was pregnant and called John. He said that he thought I was just going through a difficult time after the miscarriage and needed more time to grieve the loss. But at five months I still had that feeling, so I called John again and said, "I know you think I'm crazy, but I think I'm pregnant." He said, "Well, maybe you got pregnant again. Weirder things have happened." So I went to see him and after examining me he said, "You *are* pregnant." I said, "How far along?" And he said, "Five months!" I had no idea that I'd been pregnant with twins. In those days they didn't do routine sonograms, which would have shown two heartbeats before the miscarriage and one after. So I remember thinking, *Oh, my gosh, what if I'd had the D&C?* I would have lost the second baby without even knowing it.

After telling me how incredible this was John got very pensive and said, "Because of the medication I prescribed for you the baby may have birth defects." Both my doctor and I were Catholic, which is one of the reasons we were so close. He told me that he wouldn't perform an abortion, but that I might consider consulting with another physician and discussing this option, which I never did. I told him, and I don't think he was surprised, that I was "looking forward to having the baby and whatever gift the Lord gives me."

Through the rest of my pregnancy I was extremely worried and I prayed, "Please Lord, you've given me this child, please take care of him and protect this little boy." Then on Mother's Day, May 12, 1987, Robbie was born. John was there to deliver him and he was overjoyed and pranced around the room with this child in his arms, and said, "He's perfect! Everything about him is perfect!" And then Robbie urinated on him and John added, "Everything works!" Later, John told me that he'd kept a secret from me. He said, "The last time I delivered a baby on Mother's Day, the child was very malformed and passed away, and I didn't want to share that with you until after the birth." No wonder John had been so relieved.

I never said a word to my children about Robbie's twin, so I was shocked when Robbie asked me about his twin brother. He said, "I was a twin, wasn't I?" I'd probably pushed the memory so far down that it took me a moment before I realized what Robbie was talking about. In a way, it was so eerie.

So that's the story of my unnamed twin. But there was one other thing I told my mother when I first asked her about my brother. I said, "I know I had a brother and before he died, he gave me his speed."

CHAPTER 3

"BORDERLINE PRODIGY"

I've always been known for my "explosive speed," as any number of sports journalists have observed over the course of my career. But whether my ability to run fast comes from my twin brother, God, the universe, or just my genes, to me it was just me. So what I did on the soccer field came naturally and didn't seem at all exceptional, although I was happy to put my apparent speed to good use against my opponents.

In later years, after I'd started playing professional soccer, reporters writing about my athletic skills helped provide me with some perspective on the gifts I'd been given and when they first became evident. For example, a 2008 article in the *Columbus Dispatch* newspaper said I'd been a "borderline prodigy in soccer and judo" since I was five. What the article didn't note was that by the time I was five I'd already been kicking a soccer ball for two years and playing team soccer for one.

In the Rogers family it was inevitable that I'd be involved in sports because sports were central to my family's life even before I showed up on the scene. My two older sisters, Alicia and Nicole (Coco, for short), were already playing soccer and competing in judo before I was out of diapers. By the time I was three I often went along to soccer practice and games, and to keep myself occupied I kicked around a ball on the sidelines, running back and forth and never stopping until it was time to go home.

I don't know if it was my right-footed or left-footed kicking skills (which my father helped me hone), or just the fact that I never stopped kicking the ball that caught the eye of one of my sisters' coaches. But he approached my mom and suggested they enroll me in AYSO (American Youth Soccer Organization), even though I was only four and younger than any other players. After that, if I wasn't playing in an AYSO game, I was at home practicing my kicking or organizing neighborhood games or juggling the ball around the house. My mom and dad really encouraged me to play because they saw how good it was for me and were happy about the lessons I learned from being on a team. (Though my mom wasn't so happy the one time I kicked the ball in our living room, which was totally against the rules, and destroyed a treasured family heirloom vase—I was so upset that Mom wound up comforting *me*.)

My first team was called the Purple Octopuses, and then at the end of my first season I was recruited to the "Select" league and a team that was made up of the best players from local AYSO teams. And from there, at age seven, I got recruited to play for the South Bay Gunners, which for a time was an all-Hispanic team, except for me. (I was also two years younger than all of the other Gunners.) While soccer was an increasingly popular sport for kids my age, among Hispanic immigrants soccer was already the number one sport for boys, just as professional soccer is the number one team sport in the world (with the exception of the United States).

What I didn't know at the time was that none of this was free. My parents had to pay a fee (my mom thinks it was about $1,000) just to be on the league team, and then there was the cost of travel whenever we played a team far enough away from home that we needed to stay at a hotel. It would have been bad enough (and costly enough) if I'd been an only child and soccer had been my only sport, but until I was ten years old, soccer was just one of my two major sports, because Alicia and Coco also competed in judo. And whatever my sisters did, I had to do, too. So very quickly I joined them in class, in competitions, and then on the winners' podium.

Like my very talented sisters, I won multiple regional championships in judo. (Alicia, Coco, and I all won all three regional championships in our age groups—the triple crown—at least twice. People come from all over the country to compete at these championships, so they're actually considered national competitions even though they cover certain regions.) Between judo and soccer we got to travel all over California and from New Jersey to Hawaii and many places in between. My sisters even got to go to Japan and England, and my parents paid for it all. I can't imagine how much financial pressure that put them under, but they never said no.

With three of us playing two sports—and at some point we added my brother, Tim, and sister Katie to the mix—the daily practice and competition schedule was insane. I don't know how our parents managed it, especially since they had a joint law practice that kept them pretty busy. On a typical weekday one of my parents would leave work early (after going in at six-thirty or seven in the morning) to pick us up after school and drive us to soccer practice, then we'd get a quick dinner, and then go on to judo practice. If we were lucky, we got home by nine and then did our homework. Later, when I'd given up judo and was playing soccer for the Palos Verdes Raiders, my evenings were my own, except on those occasions when my mother would pick me up after club soccer and take me to ODP. That's the Olympic Development Program, which is a national program designed to identify young players who show skill and talent, and then develop them so there's a pool of great players for the national team to draw from.

Weekends were in some ways more intense than the weekdays because we'd all pile into the car and my parents would get us to six soccer games and a judo tournament in two days. That was even more demanding than it sounds, because those games and tournaments were typically in different places at different times. Mostly I loved it, but sometimes it got to be too much, so Timmy and I would hide our dad's car keys so we could just stay home and chill. Dad always found them.

When it came to games and competitions Mom and Dad always encouraged us to do our best, but never came down on us for losing. That didn't mean we had the option of not playing. We had to play a sport—at least one—and we had to go to practice. My parents were careful not to limit me to judo and soccer and made sure I had opportunities to try other sports, like baseball and football. I also skateboarded and surfed—I still surf.

It took me about five minutes to realize I hated both football and baseball. Mom remembers all of this a lot better than I do:

Robbie was always a talented athlete, always. When he was in intermediate school one of Robbie's coaches wanted him to play flag football because he was so fast. I went to Robbie's first formal game and he made three touchdowns. When he got off the field he said it was the stupidest game because all they do is hand you a ball and you have to run with it. He never played it again.

It was the same with Little League. When Robbie was seven or eight I enrolled him in Little League and soon after, the coach said, "This kid has real athletic talent. You should forget about soccer and judo. There's a lot of money in baseball. He's incredible on the bases." Robbie didn't like standing still, so he got very good at stealing bases. At the end of his first season, when we asked Robbie about playing the next season, he said, "Did you know that Coach So-and-so said to step in front of the ball just so I could get on the bases? I never want to play that sport again. It is so stupid. You run around the bases for a few seconds and then you stand in the middle of a field and wait for the ball to come to you." That was the end of baseball.

My sister Alicia recalls that one of the reasons I hated baseball, which isn't something I remember, was that I was so afraid of the ball hitting my "privates." She said, "During the one season Robbie played Little League, they took pictures of him and you can see he isn't really paying attention to the camera because he was so busy guarding his privates." Not surprisingly, none of these photos survive.

To me it didn't matter how many sports I was good at because from the start I was most passionate about soccer, and soccer ruled my moods. If my team won, I was happy for the week. If we lost, I'd get depressed and my mother would try to cheer me up. The best, of course, was winning a championship, and the first time that happened I was nine or ten years old and my team, the Gunners, won the State Cup.

We were the best soccer team in our age group in California and winning that championship put me on top of the world, especially since I'd scored one of the goals. After we won we were so excited that we celebrated as if we'd just won the World Cup. But we were kids and to us it probably felt better winning that championship than it did for a professional soccer player being the best in the world. I loved the competition and also loved the feeling of accomplishing something great with my team—and it was that feeling that motivated me to keep playing long after my childhood.

Early on, there were rewards that went beyond just the sheer joy of winning. My parents, especially my dad, would reward me with things if I hit certain benchmarks (which, come to think of it, probably wasn't the healthiest sort of arrangement). For example, my dad might say, "If you score six goals in a game, we'll get you a cat." I got a cat. Then he said, "If you score seven goals in a game, we'll get you a snake." I got a snake, and frogs, and toys (water guns were a favorite), and my bike.

I also learned to make deals of my own with my parents, like, "If I score today I want you to take me for sushi." I think they would have taken me anyway, but it was a nice incentive I set for myself, and my parents were happy to go along with it. (One time, when I was playing professional soccer for the Columbus Crew in 2010, I had the chance to pay my mom back and told her in advance of a game we were set to play on Mother's Day that I'd score a goal for her, which I did. We were playing against New England and that goal won the game 3–2—and it was my first goal in nearly a year!)

Beyond my passion for playing soccer, I was also a huge soccer fan, along with all the other soccer-playing kids in my neighborhood. So we constantly talked about our favorite teams and players. My favorite was Arsenal Football Club. Arsenal is an English team based in the north of London. From the first time I saw Arsenal I became a huge fan and fell in love with the way they played—at times it was almost an art form, so they were fun to watch early in the morning on television while I sat on the couch having some breakfast. Arsenal's nickname was "the Invincibles" for the 2003–2004 regular season because during that time they never lost a game in the Premier League.

Arsenal in those days was an incredible mix of guys who were very talented, including Dennis Bergkamp, Thierry Henry, Robert Pirès, Freddie Ljungberg, Nwankwo Kanu, Ashley Cole, and Gilberto Silva. They were all stars in their own ways, but Arsenal's biggest star and my favorite Arsenal player was Thierry Henry—he was fast, technical, and scored amazing goals.

But my all-time favorite player when I was growing up never played for Arsenal, and he wasn't even English. His name is Zinedine Zidane. He was a French midfielder and played for Juventus, Real Madrid, and a few other clubs; he was a true artist on the field and I hoped that one day I could be even half the soccer player he was.

Not all of my soccer friends followed a British team like I did, but most of them followed a team somewhere in the world, whether it was Italy, Spain, or Germany. It's hard to explain, but you developed a really personal relationship with your favorite team, even a continent away. Whenever we played soccer in the streets of my neighborhood, I always called my team Arsenal. And we'd play against teams named for real Arsenal opponents, like Manchester United, Liverpool, and Arsenal's biggest rival, Tottenham Hotspurs. We almost always won.

It's sort of amazing to me that I ever organized those games, because outside of sports I was a very shy child. My mother tells me that I was the kind of kid who would cling to his mother's leg when a stranger came to the house. And when she took me to school for the first time I wouldn't let go. She recalled, "Part of my heart was ripped out because that little guy . . . I'd pull one hand off and there would be an automatic flypaper reaction and his hand was right back where it started. I was finally able to peel him off me, but he was inconsolable as the teacher led him into school. So when I got to the office I called the school and fortunately by then he had settled down. He was a gentle, loving, tender child, but in moments like that my heart ached for him."

It's not like I don't recognize myself in my mother's description, because in a lot of ways I'm still shy, but when it came to sports, something happened to me and I was confident, competitive, even fearless. On the soccer field or competing in judo, no one ever got to see the child who was terrified of leaving his mother on his first day of school.

I loved competing in both soccer and judo, but it was too much. There wasn't any time to just be a kid, and when I was ten years old I told my mom I'd had enough. I said that I just couldn't do both and wanted to quit judo. I explained that I'd miss judo, but I enjoyed soccer more. Judo is an individual sport and soccer is a team sport, and I really enjoyed being part of a team. If I'd had any doubt about my decision at the time, it disappeared later when I realized soccer could help me go to college on a scholarship. But the fact that I enjoyed it more than judo really made the decision easy for me, and I never looked back.

It wasn't until later in my life that I realized all that running around had been too much for my parents, too, and for my mom in particular. In my family, we all see my mom as a powerhouse who never runs out of energy. But she's actually this tiny person—she says she's five feet tall, but I'm not so sure if she's even that tall, and she's as thin as a rail. With a full-time job and five children to look after and with all those sports to get us to and all of the money it took to keep it all going, Mom was struggling to stay above water. Of course as a child I couldn't see that anything was wrong, until my parents' marriage shattered, like a fragile treasured heirloom that got knocked to the ground by a soccer ball.

CHAPTER 4

GOLDEN BOY IN A GOLDEN FAMILY

"Your mother has moved out," my father said to me as he hung up the phone in my Aunt Leanne's condo in Chicago. This was shortly before I quit judo and I was in Chicago with my dad to compete in a tournament. Dad was in tears, but I couldn't make sense of what he was saying until he said, "Your mother wants to divorce me." I was in shock and started crying myself.

As far as I knew, my parents were happily married. It never occurred to me to think that they weren't. You ask some people whose parents divorced and they can tell you they saw it coming, that their parents argued, that they were cold toward each other, that they were like two strangers living together. Not my parents. They were masters at keeping up appearances. And I guess I was, too, because despite how upset I was when my dad broke the news to me, I won the judo tournament in

Chicago and I remember being happy about it. I don't think I was playacting, but I was able to put it in the back of my mind while I competed, which was how I dealt with just about everything that was upsetting. Throughout much of my life sports served as my escape.

To me—and, I'm guessing, to people looking in from the outside—my family was picture-perfect. And in most ways, up until that phone call, it was. My parents, while working together in the successful legal practice, were raising five athletic kids in a comfortable house next door to my grandparents (who lived in the house where my mother grew up) in Rolling Hills Estates, an affluent, semi-rural community in the hills above Los Angeles.

When people imagine the perfect Southern Californian childhood, my childhood was close to that ideal. Leaving aside the fact that we were always running from one practice or competition to the next, with never enough downtime for any of us, growing up in Rolling Hills Estates meant almost total freedom to roam and explore. Many houses were set on large pieces of land and some people kept horses, goats, and even a few cattle. Scrambling over hills, hiking along horse trails, and bushwhacking through the undergrowth, you'd never believe we were an hour's drive from downtown Los Angeles.

Rolling Hills Estates, where we'd moved when I was five (we'd been living in a working-/middle-class neighborhood in nearby San Pedro before that), is a community of eight thousand people, located in Palos Verdes, which is a peninsula in southwestern Los Angeles County. Rolling Hills Estates is just one of several little cities perched on that peninsula above

Torrance and just east of the Pacific Ocean. It's the kind of place where you can walk or ride your horse to the general store after school to buy ice cream and supplies for horses (saddles, stirrups, bridles, halters, reins, bits, harnesses) at the same time. I didn't ride when I was a child, but my mom did when she was growing up.

Like most of our neighbors, my family was socially and politically conservative and very Catholic. But because of all the sports my family was involved in, and given the range of people who came through my parents' law firm, I was fortunate to meet a lot of diverse people who weren't just like us. In some ways, my family is a bit of a contradiction. Most everyone votes Republican no matter what and is conservative in how they present themselves. But my family is also open and accepting. My mom is very loving and will hug people she has just met—my whole family is very physically demonstrative—but she goes to mass every day and she expects her children to be married before living with a partner.

I loved that my mom and dad were both very affectionate. We all did. When I was growing up, my dad loved having us on his lap, hugging us, giving us kisses. When I was really young, before we got so busy with judo and soccer, I especially liked the weekends. We'd wake up early and Dad would make breakfast for us while my brother and I watched superhero cartoons. Then my dad would take all of us for a long walk to the park in San Pedro near our house, and then on our way back we'd stop at the bakery and he'd get us a treat. Back home we'd all lie on the couch piled up together while Dad watched golf and we'd all fall asleep, Dad included.

My older sisters remember the tensions that came before my mom decided to move out, but I was too young to see it. I've since come to understand that every family has its problems and challenges whether they're visible or not, but until that phone call in Chicago I had no idea that my family was anything but perfect. And then all of a sudden we weren't.

For a short time Mom moved next door to my grandparents', and my sisters, brother, and I were sent to stay with one of my aunts up in Washington State for a few weeks. It was so strange because we went from having this intense, highly scheduled life to suddenly no schedule at all, and no one really told us what was going on. And then we moved back home and split our time between our mom's house in Rolling Hills and my dad's place in San Pedro (which was the same house we'd lived in before we moved to Rolling Hills).

For the first couple of months we switched off every week, which was way too hard for everyone, especially when you added our already packed practice and competition schedule. It was just too hectic and disorganized trying to get to school in one place and practicing in another while living in two different places at the same time. So one by one my sisters, brother, and I decided to live with our mom full-time. I know my dad was heartbroken, because he probably felt we were choosing Mom over him, but it was just easier to live in Rolling Hills with our mom, near our schools, and next door to our grandparents, which was also where our Aunt Lisa lived. We all loved Aunt Lisa, or "Lollie," as we all called her.

Aunt Lollie was my mother's youngest sibling. (My mother is the second of seven children.) And she moved back in with our grandparents to help my mom right after my parents separated. She'd been really involved in our lives from the time we were little. Before she left for Revelle College at the University of California, San Diego, she babysat my sisters. Once she was in school she'd sometimes bring us there to visit with her. After my parents separated, Aunt Lollie and my grandparents really helped keep things together.

We jokingly called Lollie "the Sergeant" because she'd gather us all up and make sure we behaved. She made very clear that she adored each of us equally, but I felt like I had a special relationship with her, which I'm guessing was how we each felt about our aunt. At that moment in my life, with my parents having a rough time, my Aunt Lollie was the most important person in the world to me. She'd come over to the house and we'd hang out on my bed and she'd ask questions about soccer and school.

And then she was gone.

There was a nighttime police chase and the woman being chased turned off her headlights. Aunt Lollie was driving through an intersection when the woman came through at 110 miles per hour, T-boning Aunt Lollie's car, killing her instantly. She was thirty-two years old.

After Aunt Lollie died, I talked to her a lot in my prayers, saying that I hoped she was with God and was being well taken care of. To this day I miss her terribly, and a couple of years ago I got a tattoo on the inside of my bicep in memory of her.

If my family wasn't what it seemed once you looked below the surface, then neither was Rolling Hills Estates, and the older I got, the more clear that became. The most obvious evidence that things were not quite as they seemed were the parties and the drugs. I started going to parties the summer after eighth grade. These were insane parties, unlike anything I've ever been to since. They were always somewhere in Palos Verdes at someone's giant mansion while their parents were away for the weekend or on vacation. Imagine four hundred kids in togas, a live band playing music, kegs of beer, and people doing drugs, just like you've seen in the movies. It was all these kids with too much money, having fun and getting into trouble with absolutely no adult supervision. It wasn't like I didn't drink, too, although I was a quick learner, so it only took getting sick a couple of times to discover my limits. But I didn't do drugs, other than trying pot a few times, which made me tired, anxious, and paranoid.

I was definitely *not* one of those unsupervised kids, and after my mom saw what went on with my two older sisters at Peninsula High School and heard about all the trouble other teenagers in our community were getting into, she decided to send me forty miles east to live with my cousins in Huntington Beach so I could attend Mater Dei, a private Catholic school. It happened to be a more convenient place for me to live because of where I had to go for soccer practice, but that wasn't the primary reason my mother sent me there. She just wanted me far away from Peninsula High School, and I don't think she minded that Mater Dei conducted routine drug tests.

When my mother first told me she wanted me to go to Mater Dei, I was outraged (in the way only a teenager can be outraged at his mother) because I didn't want to leave all of my friends who were going to Peninsula, and besides, I complained to my mother, my sisters were both going there, too. It just wasn't fair. But then I went to visit Mater Dei and thought it was a really cool school with a nice campus. And much to my surprise I wound up loving it—the history, the tradition, the school pride, all the school activities, the football games, and even the school uniforms. I'd wear khaki, gray, or blue shorts with a navy blue, maroon, or gray polo shirt, with a pair of Converse or Vans sneakers. This made it easy to dress well, because everyone had to dress in the same kinds of clothes. I've always liked dressing well, but I'm also Californian, so I like my clothes to be casual.

After a year of living with my cousins I moved in with my soccer coach's parents, Gene and Luanne Theslof. (My coach, who was also one of my first mentors, was Nick Theslof.) And that turned out to be perfect because I wasn't driving yet and Nick could take me to all of my trainings and games. By then Nick had invited me to play with the Orange County Blue Star, a Professional Development League team that he coached, in addition to my club team, the Palos Verdes Raiders. Most of my teammates on Blue Star were college players from the local area, which was a lot of fun because I got to play with guys who were a lot better than I was, but I could still outrun them. So it was a chance to learn a lot and also to show off a bit to guys who had a lot more experience than I did. This included Jürgen Klinsmann, a legendary German footballer who played for a time with Blue Star using the alias "Jay Göppingen" (and in

2011 was named head coach of the U.S. men's national soccer team).

My mom always seemed to know what was best for me. And lucky for me, at that age I didn't have a choice about doing what she said.

I think one of the lessons you learn growing up is that things are usually a lot more complicated than they look on the surface. Just because something seems golden, like your family or your community, doesn't mean that once you scrape away that shiny outer layer things will look as good underneath. And the same could be said for me when I was a teenager, because, just like my family and the community in which I grew up, I looked pretty golden, until you scratched the surface. In fact, if you were to ask my brother and sisters, they would tell you that in our family I was the golden child who almost always got his way. From the outside I was a stereotypical, all-American boy who was into sports, never got into trouble, and was nice to his grandparents.

I have to admit that with all the attention I got and all the success I had in judo and later in soccer, I felt pretty golden. Some people who knew me might have thought I was a bit spoiled. Then as I grew into my teens I began to understand that while I may have felt golden and looked pretty golden to the people around me, I had this one huge flaw. And from everything I'd learned up to that point in my life I knew that if I ever let anyone see my flaw I'd be guaranteed disappointment, condemnation, and maybe even rejection from my family, friends, God, and the soccer community.

Yet long before *I* came to the realization that I had anything to hide, those who knew me best could already tell that I was different from other young boys. They could sense that little Robbie Rogers, who loved his bow ties, vests, and dress shorts— and notwithstanding his status as a soccer and judo prodigy— was a "fairy."

CHAPTER 5

YOU'VE GOT TO BE CAREFULLY TAUGHT

You don't grow up hating yourself by accident. You don't learn to lie about your true nature on a whim. You don't pretend to be straight just for the fun of it. You have to learn and be taught these things and I was a good student.

There's a song from the 1949 Rodgers & Hammerstein musical *South Pacific* called "You've Got to Be Carefully Taught" that reminds me of my experience growing up. The first line of the song is, "You've got to be taught to hate and fear." The lyrics go on to talk about prejudice and describe how children are taught to hate people who are different from them and to hate all the people their relatives hate.

My family and church would never have tolerated the kind of prejudice described in the Rodgers & Hammerstein song. But gay people were another story, and growing up I heard and saw plenty that made me think that being gay was bad, defective, and sinful. I guess if you're straight and taught to hate gay people that's not as big a problem, because then you don't grow up hating *yourself*, although teaching children to hate anyone is wrong and I think deeply held prejudice of any kind is soul-destroying. But when you teach a child who is gay (or lesbian, bisexual, or transgender) that his fundamental nature is somehow bad, you create a situation where that child grows up hating himself and feels compelled to hide his true feelings, no matter what the cost is to him and those around him. And that's what happened to me beginning in early childhood.

Just a quick disclaimer before I say anything more: My parents did not set out to knowingly hurt me. They were taught by their parents and church to believe certain things about homosexuality and gay people that were widely held beliefs at the time. My goal in sharing my experiences with you is not to trash them (or other family members, or teammates, or friends), but to give you insight into my experience growing up as a gay kid in a world that was filled with hate and prejudice. It was a world in which I learned to hide anything about myself that might have given anyone any idea that I wasn't the All-American Straight Golden Boy they wanted to believe I was—and that I desperately wanted to be.

It all started with *My Little Pony*, a cartoon TV program I liked to watch when I was a very young boy. The show was built around a cast of characters based on the colorful and highly decorated plastic pony toys manufactured by Hasbro. I can't tell you why I loved *My Little Pony*, but I did. (Ironically, my favorite pony was the blue one with wings and a rainbow-colored mane and tail—for those who don't know, the rainbow flag is a symbol of gay pride.) The fact that I loved *My Little*

Pony in the first place was the problem, because the *My Little Pony* TV show and the My Little Pony dolls that I collected and played with were designed for and marketed to girls.

I have to give my mom some credit because when I asked for My Little Pony dolls for Christmas and birthday gifts (and we each got to pick out a new toy when another sibling was born), she let me choose whatever I wanted. And what I always wanted was a My Little Pony doll and another less-than-masculine toy, this stuffed dog that had a flap on its belly with little puppies inside.

But I don't want to give my mother—or my sisters—too much credit, because they liked to tease me about the fact that I liked to play with toys that most boys had no interest in. They used to sing a song meant to torment me about *"My Little Pony* and baloney,"* and they'd sing it back and forth until I started crying. I was very sensitive when I was a child (I still am), so it didn't take a lot to get me to cry. Still, I don't remember the teasing bothering me all that much. Though apparently it's not that way for every boy who loves *My Little Pony.* I recently read about an eleven-year-old boy who was a fan of the *My Little Pony* cartoon show and was teased so relentlessly that he tried to take his own life, which is beyond heartbreaking.

Other than the occasional teasing, my sisters were happy to play dolls with me. And my mother was content to let us enjoy ourselves. My father was another story, and on a few occasions when I was very young he made it clear that he didn't like his namesake playing with "girlie things." I remember one time overhearing him say to my mother in a really angry voice, "I don't *ever* want to see him playing with dolls again! I don't want a fairy for a son!"

It would be years before I understood that the word "fairy"

was a stand-in for "fag" or "homosexual" and that my father was afraid that by playing with dolls I'd grow up to be gay. What was clear from my father's tone of voice was that whatever kind of fairy he didn't want me to be, I figured it had to be pretty bad. After that my mother deftly shifted me away from My Little Pony dolls and over to more standard toy horses, which she would buy for me at the general store. Happily for everyone, as I got older and my brother Tim and I spent more time playing together, we only wanted toys that would shoot stuff. We'd set up little soldiers and go at it the way boys were supposed to play. That must have come as a huge relief to my father.

There was one other gender-bending thing I did as a child that made my dad insanely angry, and his reaction is burned into my memory as if imprinted there by a red-hot branding iron. My two older sisters and I liked to dress up and play a game they called "Cool Girls." I was pretty young when we did this, so my sister Alicia has more complete memories of this than I do. Here's what she remembers:

> My mom and dad both worked full-time and went on a lot of trips together, so after school and when they were away we stayed with Hilda, our adopted grandmother. She was the most amazing, loving, good woman and we were so blessed to have known her. We went to garage sales with her and we'd buy 1950s lingerie and other silky things. Then we'd come home and Hilda would do up my hair and Coco's hair in little curls. We'd put on these slips we'd bought and Robbie would, too—he did whatever we did. So we'd get dressed up—I chose the

name Sara and Robbie's name was Robin and Coco was someone else—and we'd parade around the house and pretend we were cool girls.

One time we were playing in Hilda's back room when my dad walked in—he was just back from a trip or came by early to pick us up to take us home. He took one look at Robbie all dressed up and I could see him getting really angry because he was grinding his teeth. He didn't raise his voice very often, but when he did it was scary. He yelled, "My son will not be a faggot!" Robbie just froze. We all did. I remember the look of shock on Robbie's face, and his furrowed brow just beneath his perfect bowl haircut.

When I talked with my mom about this recently she recalled being at Hilda's house that day, too, and that dad also yelled at Hilda and said, "Don't let my son dress up like a faggot!" Here's what Mom remembers:

Rob was out-of-control angry and I told him that he couldn't yell at the children like that and he said, "He's going to grow up to be a fairy." And I said, "I don't care what he's going to grow up to be. You may not do this." I felt that as a mother I had to step in and say, "You're not going to do this to our son. He will be who he is, and if he wants to play like this with his sisters, don't you ever yell at him like that." Robbie's facial expression changed dramatically when his father yelled at him and he appeared extremely hurt.

That experience with our dad just taught us to be more careful when we played "Cool Girls," because it wasn't like we stopped. There was another time when my dad caught us and this time it was at home when we were still living in San Pedro. Alicia was probably eight, Coco was six, and I was four. We'd raided my mother's closet and used her scarves and whatever else we could find to make togas. I put a shirt on my head and pretended that I had long hair. We were on the second floor playing and running around and having a lot of fun, which probably explains why we didn't hear Dad coming up the stairs, but suddenly he was screaming at us. I was so scared that I have no memory of exactly what he said or what I said in response, but Alicia remembers that I said, "I'm pretending to be a horse. I'm not pretending to be a girl."

I have no idea how I knew to say that, but apparently I knew enough to know that what made my dad so upset was that his little boy was pretending to be a girl. As I came to understand much later, in Dad's mind that meant I'd grow up to be gay, which was something so terrible that the thought of it made his blood boil. (My father is now so supportive and pro-gay that it's hard to imagine he ever had any problem with me playing with dolls or dressing up to play "Cool Girls.") Of course, not all boys who play with dolls and play dress-up with their sisters turn out to be gay, but this boy did. And if there are any parents out there who still worry that their child's choice of toys has an impact on the child's sexuality, let me put your minds at ease. There is no cause-and-effect. Don't forget, I also liked to play soccer and was a judo champion, and that didn't make me straight.

Before I figured out what "fairy" or "faggot" meant, or that it had anything to do with my sexuality, I had a sense that I was different from other boys. In elementary school I'd hear my friends talk about girlfriends and I couldn't relate to it. I wasn't excited about the idea of having a girlfriend and couldn't understand why they *were*. I thought that maybe I was just afraid, but at first I couldn't put my finger on what the problem was.

One time, I remember watching an episode of *Dawson's Creek* on television and seeing a gay character, Jack McPhee, and I really took notice. It wasn't that I was attracted to Jack—at least I don't recall being attracted to him. There was just something about his character that felt familiar, that Jack and I shared more in common than simply his hair and eye color. But even before *Dawson's Creek*, when I watched movies or TV shows I was always more attracted to the guy characters than the girl characters and didn't know why. Then, as I got older and realized that I was gay and understood why I was attracted to them, I didn't allow myself to have those feelings.

Maybe it sounds crazy, but I never really let myself feel attracted to other guys. It felt too dangerous. I told myself that I could never date one of my teammates, or any soccer player, any friend—anyone I found even remotely attractive, for that matter. I trained myself to say no, no, no to any feelings of attraction I might have had even before they surfaced. For most of my life, when I saw a good-looking guy it was like looking at a sibling, so I'd feel sick to my stomach if I allowed so much as a flicker of attraction to slip through.

My growing sense that something was wrong with me came at around the same time (in 1997) that the character Ellen Morgan (played by Ellen DeGeneres) on the sitcom *Ellen* told the world she was gay. More than forty million people watched that episode (by comparison, the top-rated *Modern Family* was watched by around ten million viewers in a typical week in 2013). I can't imagine that my family watched *Ellen* or that episode, but even if we had I don't think I would have made any connection between what was going on with me and what Ellen Morgan (and Ellen DeGeneres herself) announced to the world.

When I was ten or eleven I also started to hear gay slur words and kids would say, "Don't be so gay," like gay was a bad thing, like you were doing something stupid. While I knew by then what gay people were, I can't say I had a real understanding yet that I was gay myself—or at least I wasn't willing to consider that possibility. But somewhere deep down I must have known because my ears perked up whenever I heard those slurs or heard about gay civil right issues on the news or debated by my family or discussed at church.

What I heard at church cut especially deep, because I didn't want to lead a sinful life. My understanding from Sunday sermons and from CCD class (Confraternity of Christian Doctrine class—Sunday school for Catholics) was that there was no place for homosexuality, that it was a sin, that it was evil. You couldn't live that lifestyle and go to heaven. What was a bit confusing for me was that there were lots of things in the Bible that you weren't supposed to do, but for some reason that no one seemed to explain, homosexuality was a really bad one and I wasn't about to ask why.

My parents would discuss gay stuff occasionally. It wasn't a big talking point, but when same-sex marriage came up, my parents (and later my mother and her second husband) would say that marriage was between a man and a woman. They never bashed gay people, but they talked about marriage being a holy union between a man and a woman and how that was in the Bible. Polygamy and incest are sins, too, but homosexuality was somehow worse. They'd talk about what would happen if gays got married, that it was going to change all kinds of things and somehow undermine traditional families and lead to crazy stuff, like people marrying their pets.

The one time my mother said something that made me think she was really anti-gay was so incidental, at least for her, that she doesn't remember it. But I do. Vividly. I was probably thirteen or fourteen years old at the time and we were driving in my mom's Toyota 4Runner on our way to a sushi place she knew I liked in Torrance. That was one of the great things about my mom: she always found a way to spend time with each of her children independently. So that evening it was just the two of us.

We had the radio on and there was an Elton John song playing—I don't remember which one—and just as we were crossing the Pacific Coast Highway Mom said something like, "I used to love Elton John until he got all weird and gay," or "I really like that song, but it's too bad he's gay." I thought, *Gosh,*

COMING OUT TO PLAY

my mom really said that? Elton John is one of the most talented musicians of our time, but then she finds out he's gay and now she doesn't like him?

I loved Elton John's music. He's a great singer-songwriter and his music is something that makes you feel good. I always thought he was gay but that wasn't an issue for me, and I didn't see how his being gay could be a problem for anyone, but clearly it was for my mom. That really scared me. It made me think I could never say anything to my mother about what I already suspected about myself because she would think there was something wrong with me, too. We listened to the rest of the song in silence.

The only person in my family who ever spoke positively about gay people was my Aunt Angel, my dad's sister. As I found out later, she suspected I was gay and wanted to make a point of letting me know that it was okay if I was. She lived in Florida and still does, so I didn't see her often, but over the years when I visited with her she would talk about her gay friends and say positive things about them so I would know it was okay with her. She was always clear that she didn't care whether someone was gay or straight. But I was totally clueless that this had anything to do with me, especially since my aunt would also ask me if I was dating any girls. I just assumed that if she knew I was gay she would never have asked about that.

It was really thoughtful of my aunt to try to let me know it was okay with her that I was gay, but later, once she knew I was gay, I explained why I never confided in her. I said, "Angel, you could have said anything to me about gay people. It wouldn't have made me feel any better and I still wouldn't have felt comfortable telling you. It was about me and what I thought about myself, not what you thought about me." The sad truth was that I was so badly scarred by then, it didn't matter what anyone else said. For me it was an internal battle and I couldn't recognize when someone who loved me reached out to let me know that she accepted me for who I was. I had to come to terms with myself first. I had to recognize and accept that I wasn't a bad person and that God put me on this earth for a purpose and not just to suffer.

While no one thing set me on the path to keeping silent about my sexuality, there was one experience that helped crystallize for me how painfully difficult it was going to be to reconcile Robbie Rogers the up-and-coming soccer player with Robbie Rogers the undeniably gay teenager. Before I explain my tortured reconciliation, I want to tell you about that crystallizing experience, which came during my sophomore year of high school, when I was invited to train with the U-17 (under age seventeen) national team at the elite IMG Academy in Bradenton, Florida, along with forty of the best young soccer players in the country. For the players who were ultimately selected to be on the U-17 national team, you got to compete against other national teams in your age group from around the world.

Even though it meant leaving Mater Dei, it was incredibly exciting to be invited to attend the Bradenton residency, but I almost didn't go. First, because my mom objected to me going; she thought it wouldn't be good for me to be away from the family. (She was right, and she wasn't the only one—Jürgen

Klinsmann, who was someone I looked up to and had become one of my mentors, thought it would be better if I was around my family, in an environment that was loving and supportive.) And, second, I almost *couldn't* go because I'd developed a problem with my knee that made it excruciating for me to walk, let alone run. Here's what my mom remembers from that time:

Robbie developed some problems associated with his muscles and his bones growing at different rates. I got him into physical therapy, and it was a long and difficult process for him to recover. One time when we were coming back from physical therapy he started crying. I pulled over to the side of the road and asked him, "What's wrong?" And he said, "I may not get to be a professional soccer player and I want this with my whole heart. This is the first time I ever realized what it would be like in my life not to have soccer."

So Robbie and I wound up making a deal about his going to Bradenton because I could see how important it was to him. Robbie had been on board when I originally said no to the residency program, but during this conversation Robbie made another pitch for going. He said, "Look, if I'm going to do this, if I'm going to be a professional soccer player, I need to go to Bradenton." So we made that our goal, to get him 100% healthy, and if we got to that point, then I would let him attend Bradenton after all. And he did it, working as hard as anyone, going to physical therapy three or four times a week, until he was fit and ready to go.

Bradenton turned out to be like *Lord of the Flies*. It was brutal going to class with, training with, living with, and being surrounded by my teammates twenty-four hours a day, seven days a week. These were guys who were always calling each other "faggot" and talking about girls in the most demeaning ways, using language I couldn't imagine using about anyone (and couldn't imagine repeating here). Both on and off the field I found myself swimming in a soup of raging male hormones.

Even if I'd been straight I couldn't have imagined talking about girls the way my teammates did. I realized that they were fifteen-year-olds talking the way they thought grown men talked about women, and were just trying to live up to the stereotype. But it wasn't like I could say to myself that they were just feeling the same things I felt for guys, because I'd done such a good job of burying my feelings that I really had no visceral sense of how I felt about guys. I mostly felt nothing.

I can look back now and see that it was just a pack mentality, that when the guys were all together they turned into a bunch of hungry and horny wolves. When you got them on their own they were much more chill, as if they'd taken some sort of antidote that turned them back into teenage boys. But back then it made me feel totally different and completely isolated because I couldn't understand what they were feeling.

Even worse than all the talk about girls was the number of times each day I heard "that's so gay" or "fag" or "faggot," and it wasn't like any of our coaches or teachers ever said anything to stop it. The slurs weren't directed at anyone who was gay, but they were always said maliciously and felt like a punch in the chest every time I heard them. But I couldn't react. I couldn't give any indication that those words meant any more to me than they did to anyone else, or I'd risk someone figuring out why I cared.

What really got to me was the fact that I could never escape from it. There was no life away from soccer, so what should have been the best time in my life—a time when I got increasing recognition for my skills as a soccer player on a bigger and bigger stage—turned out to be really difficult. I was so unhappy off the field that it affected my game *on* the field, which was something I knew I'd have to overcome if I was going to fulfill my dream of becoming a professional soccer player. To make things worse, I couldn't share how I was feeling with my family and began to withdraw from them in a way that left my mother, in particular, confused. I told myself that I couldn't tell my mother how miserable I was because then she'd ask me why I felt that way. And I could never tell her. Never.

Coming off the semester in Bradenton, I could see that there was only one path for me to follow if I was going to continue playing soccer. There was no question in my mind that soccer was my life and that I wanted more than anything to turn pro. Although I didn't think of it this way at the time, soccer had become my identity. I was Robbie Rogers the talented soccer player and I got lots of strokes for that—from coaches, from other players, and perhaps most importantly, from my family. (I knew I wasn't going to get those strokes if I was Robbie Rogers not-the-soccer-player or gay Robbie Rogers the average high school student.) And there was another thing soccer did for me. Playing soccer actually helped me forget that underneath the surface I was this shameful and sinful person nobody would love. On the field I could push all those bad feelings aside and still experience the joy that came from stepping onto the field with some of the best young athletes in the country who loved soccer as much as I did.

When I looked around to figure out what I was going to do, it wasn't hard to see that there weren't any gay professional soccer players. As far as I knew there were no openly gay men playing professional team sports anywhere in the world, and that left me with only one option: suppress my feelings, pretend to be straight, pray to God to take these bad feelings away, and never share with another single human being the truth about my sexuality.

All I wanted at that age was to be like everyone else, and while I still held out hope that somehow I could figure out how I could make myself straight by praying harder or maybe even meeting the right girl, in the meantime I would put a lid on myself and seal it so securely that there was never any danger of slipping and letting someone discover I was gay. Of course, when you're fifteen or sixteen years old, you have no idea what it means to keep such a tightly held secret about something as powerful and instinctive as your sexuality. It would take me years to realize what a painful, lonely, and ultimately impossible path I'd chosen.

After one semester at IMG I'd had enough and decided to go back to California for my junior and senior years of high school while I continued to play for the national teams in my age group. (By then my mother had moved the family south to Huntington

Beach in Orange County, so I went to Huntington High School.) At least at home I could get time by myself to recover and recharge. One lesson I'd learned from the semester away was that if I was going to successfully keep a part of myself hidden, I couldn't do it in a place far from home surrounded by other guys my age twenty-four hours a day; I needed personal downtime to relax, recharge, and get rid of at least some of the toxic feelings that came along with leading a pretend life.

When I decided after Bradenton that the only way to deal with my sexuality was to keep a lid on my feelings, it didn't occur to me that sooner or later I was going to have to deal with girls. Girls liked soccer players, and soccer players were supposed to want to have sex with them, and by my junior year of high school the pressure on me to have sex with girls had grown to the point where I felt like I had no choice if I was going to keep people from getting suspicious. And the truth is, I was also curious to see what would happen. Would I like it? Would having sex with a girl make me want it more? I didn't want it at all, so if having sex with a girl made me want it even a little bit that would be a big deal. Would it take away the feelings of attraction I had for men? I told myself that I couldn't know until I tried.

Long before high school, girls had made it clear that they were interested in me. In fourth and fifth grades, girls would follow me around and they'd write letters to me saying, "You're so cute." It wasn't a surprise that by failing to express an interest in girls I would attract another kind of attention that I didn't want. At Miraleste Intermediate School in Rancho Palos Verdes, I had a friend, a girl, who said, "So many girls like you and you never date any girls. Do you think maybe you're gay?" I didn't know at that time if I was gay, but it really scared me and made me feel defensive. All I managed to say was "We're in sixth grade! What do you mean?" Luckily we weren't actually talking face-to-face because we were exchanging messages on AOL, so she couldn't see how shocked I was.

A few months later I started to date a girl I thought was pretty. We'd hang out, go to the movies, and write each other notes. I knew deep down that I was just trying to prove I wasn't gay, although it was also confusing because I'd think, *She is really pretty and maybe I* do *like her.* But as I got older, I realized that finding a girl attractive and liking her weren't the same thing as being sexually attracted, that this was just me thinking a girl was pretty and that I should date her because that's what guys my age were supposed to do.

By my junior year in high school you couldn't get away with just talking to girls on AOL and hanging out. If I was going to seem normal I was going to have to prove myself by actually having sex with a girl. It wasn't anything I planned, but one time when I was staying with my coach's family two girls came over after school. They were good friends, so it didn't occur to me that I'd hook up with either of them. We hung out for a while in the Jacuzzi and had a few beers. Then one of them left and the girl who stayed behind went up to my room with me and we started kissing. I still wasn't thinking we were going to have sex, but we did.

After the fact, I didn't want to hang out with her, but the sex itself wasn't bad. For the next few weeks she called me again and again, hitting me up, wanting to get together again. I kept avoiding her because having sex once with a girl was more than enough for me. And besides, I knew that the other kids at school would hear I'd had sex with a girl, so I'd achieved my goal of giving the impression that I wasn't gay. At least for now.

For someone who is straight it probably sounds strange to hear me complain about girls being attracted to me and wanting to have sex with me, because that's the totally normal thing. But for me sex with a girl was so *not* normal. It wasn't what I wanted, and all that attention from girls just reinforced the feeling that there was something really wrong with me.

These days, when I've been asked by guys what the problem is for me having sex with girls, I ask them to imagine that they live in a world where almost everyone is gay and being straight is a bad thing. I say, "Imagine that all the movies you see and the songs you hear celebrate same-sex love and the people around you are always talking about hooking up with someone of the same sex. In your heart of hearts you know that you're straight, but to prove you're gay—and so no one figures out that you're really straight and rejects you—you have to fake being attracted to guys and you need to have sex with them just to prove you're normal. And now imagine that you have to marry a guy and have sex with him over and over again for the rest of your life." Imagine.

CHAPTER 6

COLLEGE MAN

What would you say to someone who said, "If you don't hook up with a girl by the weekend, you're gay"? Well, during afternoon training a couple of weeks into my first semester at the University of Maryland, that's exactly what one of my soccer teammates, a senior, said to me. I hadn't hooked up with anyone during the first few weeks of school and didn't know that anyone was keeping track. I'm sure I just laughed at what he said, but inside my head I was screaming, *Oh, gosh! Is that the impression I'm giving off? Does he really think I'm gay? Or is he just messing with me?* Whatever he might have meant, I took it to mean that I'd better hook up with a girl by the weekend or my teammates would think I was gay.

If it had been up to me the University of Maryland at College Park wouldn't have even been on my list of potential schools because UCLA had been recruiting me for a long time and was my first choice. Believe it or not, the college recruiting process started during my freshman year of high school. That year I must have received thirty or forty letters from soccer scouts and college head coaches who had been keeping an eye on me while I played on youth national teams and in club tournaments.

By then I'd developed a reputation for being a speedy, technical, and dangerous winger. For those who aren't familiar with soccer, a winger's primary goal is to run at the opposing fullbacks while you look for opportunities to score a goal by crossing or creating chances for yourself. When you're a winger, speed is essential, and so is the ability to dribble the ball while you pick out the perfect cross. I wound up with offers of full scholarships from a long list of good schools, including UCLA, the University of Virginia, and Boston College.

If it had been *totally* up to me I wouldn't have gone to college at all. Even after I agreed with my mom to go for a year (she remembers it differently and says that I made a commitment to go for two, which I probably conveniently forgot), I was still thinking I'd skip college and go to the Netherlands to play for one of two Dutch clubs, Heerenveen or PSV Eindhoven.

It wasn't like I came up with these ideas on my own. While my mom was in one corner arguing for college, "the men in your life," as she referred to them—my dad and some of my coaches—were arguing for Europe. Here's what my mother recalls, and she remembers better than I do because she could see the whole thing playing out from ten thousand feet up. I was in the middle of it and not really aware of the battle of the wills between the adults:

> My feeling was that every person needs the experience of a university. Because that's where you find yourself. You can be a soccer player at the university, you can be a writer, you can be a botanist. You get to explore your interests and meet other people from different walks of life. Robbie was a teenager and I saw his time at the university as precious years during which he could develop into a well-rounded young man. But the men in his life were telling him, "No, you need to go to Europe. That's where fame and fortune is. You're not going to learn anything at the university, because the level of play there is so inferior." Of course I'm paraphrasing and giving it my tilt, but Robbie was being pulled in that direction, so my job as the mom was to counterbalance the men and pull Robbie back. I didn't feel that the men had Robbie's best long-term interests at heart and believed that I did.

From my perspective my coaches were opening up a whole world to me. For example, during my sophomore year of high school Jürgen Klinsmann set up an opportunity for me to play with the youth team for Bayern Munich in Germany, which I did, and I loved it. And then in my junior and senior years Nick Theslof arranged for me to go over to Holland for a couple of months to train with PSV Eindhoven, with their reserve team and their youth team. (Nick had played with PSV when he was younger, so he had connections at the club.) The second time, which was at the start of 2005, I'd finished up at Huntington High School a semester early, so I was free to go, but Mom set some conditions. Again, here's what my mom remembers:

By this point we'd already met with Sasho Cirovski, the coach from the University of Maryland, who desperately wanted Robbie on his team. This man is incredible, a total alpha male. You have to scrape him off the ceiling. Sasho called me from Maryland and said, "Don't sign anything. I'm flying out tomorrow. I'm going to form my team around Robbie. I know him, I've seen him, I've scouted him. Promise me you won't sign anything. I'll be there tomorrow morning."

Sasho had such high energy I thought I was going to get electrocuted through the phone. I said, "You've got my ear, I promise I won't do anything until we break bread." And true to his word, as always, he flew out from Maryland and was here the next morning. We went to a sandwich place in Newport and seated at the table were Nick Theslof, Sasho, me, and Robbie. Sasho was a tsunami and very quickly had me convinced that Maryland could be the right place for Robbie, but I knew Robbie was thinking, *I'm going to tell Mom I'm going to college, but I'm really not.*

Mom was right, because that's what I was thinking. So she made a deal with me in the secret hope that I'd go see the University of Maryland and fall in love with it. She said I could go to Holland only if, when I was in Europe, I signed up to take the SAT exam. I hadn't been in a rush to take the SAT because I figured I didn't need to if I was turning pro, and if I wound up going to college instead I didn't think I'd need SAT scores if I was going to school on a sports scholarship. I protested and said that I didn't think you could take the SAT in Europe, but Mom said I had no choice and that she'd arrange it, which she did. Clearly she wasn't giving up without a fight. And I wanted to go to Holland, so I agreed to Mom's terms.

At the same time, Sasho persuaded me to stop in Maryland on my way to Europe to meet the guys on the team, which I knew would make my mother happy, so I agreed to that as well. I still thought it was a waste of time to stop in Maryland, but then I arrived on campus and it was like something out of the movies—red-brick buildings with white columns all set on beautiful lawns. UCLA is nice, but it's not like that. I was there for three days and met all the guys on the soccer team, the Maryland Terrapins (the Terps, for short), who were easy to get along with and made me feel really welcome. I spent a lot of time with Sasho and the coaching staff. They took me around the campus, through the classroom buildings, and to the stadium. And they talked with me about my goals and what I hoped to achieve playing for Maryland. After the first day I was sold and called home. I said to my mom, "I love this school. If I go to school I want to go here." I was confident that if I went there it would be a great experience and that I'd be successful there in the way I wanted to be. The University of Maryland also happened to be a good school, but reading and studying at that age weren't as important to me as they are now, so I really didn't care about that.

From Maryland I flew to the Netherlands and spent the next

two months training and playing in Eindhoven. It's a cool city and I could ride my bike to training—and it was the best training I could hope to get anywhere in the world—then I'd come home and have the rest of the day to do what I wanted. I was a bit lonely, but I had some friends on the team and would meet them after practice and we'd walk around the city. From my time there it was easy to imagine living in Europe, but I wound up not getting any serious offers from European professional soccer teams. So it was a good thing my mother had arranged for me to take the SAT, which I wound up doing in Amsterdam, because once I said yes to Maryland, the first thing they asked for were my SAT scores. Mom was right again, but fortunately she's not the kind of person to ever say, "I told you so."

From the Netherlands I flew directly to Florida to attend a U-20 national team training camp. I'd been invited by the team's coach, Sigi Schmid—I'd known Sigi since I was eight years old. His son Kyle and I were good friends on the Gunners, my youth club team. Sigi would come and watch all of our games, and we'd often go to LA Galaxy games together. Then after national team training camp I went home to California to get ready to leave for the University of Maryland. Unfortunately, by the time I got home, after months of intense training and playing, I was having a lot of trouble with my knee.

My knee hadn't been right since I'd had surgery on it the year before, and now it was swelling up almost every day after practice and games and I was in a lot of pain, which meant I couldn't play at my best. That surgery hadn't been so bad, but the recovery had been awful. I'd been diagnosed with osteo-chondritis, which is a rare knee problem (although not uncommon in adolescent athletes because of all the stress we put on our joints) where the end of the thighbone, the femur, gets damaged and doesn't heal properly. I'd been warned that if I didn't have the surgery and continued playing, I could do permanent damage to my knee and might never walk again, so it wasn't like I had a choice.

I had the surgery during the summer of 2004, and afterward I had to be in a wheelchair for six weeks, because I wasn't allowed to put any weight on the knee, and then had to be on crutches for weeks. It was really depressing when I went back to Huntington High School in September for my final semester and couldn't play soccer at all. I was in rehab for months before I started playing again in 2005, and by the time I left to see the University of Maryland, and then went on to the Netherlands for two months, I was in pretty good shape, although the swelling continued to be a problem.

So come August, after packing my bags, I flew across the country with my mom and Tim and Katie for orientation at the University of Maryland, hoping the whole time that if I kept icing my knee and taking care of it, it would get better on its own, but I couldn't even get through our first exhibition game. I somehow managed to play for the first twenty minutes, but that was it. Running was excruciating and after those twenty minutes I could hardly walk.

I was lucky that my mother was with me. She and Katie and Tim planned to stay a few days to help me get settled (and Mom wanted Katie and Tim to see where their older brother was going to school). Sasho, my new coach, took me right from the exhibition game to the team doctor's house. He examined my knee, which was pretty swollen, and sent me for an MRI. At the hospital the doctor explained to my mom and me what the problem was—that there wasn't enough clearance between the kneecap and the femur, so the kneecap was rubbing against the femur, cutting off the blood supply to that bone. Apparently my knee hadn't healed properly after the first surgery and now I was going to need another operation. I was in tears because I couldn't believe I had to do this all over again.

What worried me about having surgery for a second time was the possibility—the fear—that I wouldn't recover to the point where I could be the kind of soccer player people expected me to be and I wanted to be. That was my identity. It's who I was. Everything I did, all of the people I knew, and all the praise I got were connected to soccer. If I didn't play soccer at the level I'd been playing, how would I go to college? If I was washed up, it wasn't like the University of Maryland was going to give me a scholarship for my brilliant academic record. Without soccer, what was my purpose in life?

But Sasho was very reassuring. He said, "We're going to take care of this." A couple of days later I went in for surgery and then my teammates came to the hospital to take me back to the hotel where my mom was staying, because she wanted to look after me. That evening Sasho stopped by to talk to my mother. He said, "You really don't know me, but Robbie is now part of our family. You can stay in Maryland as long as you want. But we're going to take over, we're going to take care of him, and he'll be back on the field in no time."

With that reassurance, my mom, Tim, and Katie went home

and I got to work getting back on my feet. Sasho was true to his word, because they really took care of everything. During my recovery, Sasho had me stay with our captain, Michael Dellorusso, at his apartment. This time I didn't have to be in a wheelchair, just crutches for several weeks. I did rehab in Baltimore every day, or would do rehab with the physical therapists at Maryland. Within two weeks I was in a pool running on a treadmill and I was back training with the team long before I could have imagined, and only missed the first two games of the season.

Sasho turned out to be the perfect coach for me because he really cared. That's something he demonstrated to my family and me from the start. Once I was back training and playing, I found Sasho to be the kind of coach who encouraged me to work harder and do better, which was exactly what I needed.

It was a couple of weeks after I went back to training with the Terps that my teammate, totally out of the blue, said that if I didn't hook up with a girl that weekend I was gay. Looking back now, I wish I'd said in response: "Don't be stupid. I'll hook up with a girl if I want to hook up with a girl. And besides, having sex with a girl doesn't prove you're straight. Or don't you know that?" But I was too afraid and too young to say anything remotely close to that. I didn't even think it.

You have to wonder what was going through this guy's head to say that kind of thing to a freshman. I have no idea, but I can tell you what was going through *my* head. I was totally panicked and decided I'd better hook up with a girl that coming weekend to prove that I wasn't gay. Just writing about this story makes me feel so sad to think that I felt like I had no choice but to have sex with a girl to prove that I wasn't gay. I feel sad for my eighteen-year-old self and I feel sad for the girl I had sex with, because the truth is I was using her and that was clearly wrong.

Finding a girl to hook up with didn't exactly take work because there were a lot of girls who wanted to hook up with the soccer players. That weekend, after the game, we had a party in our suite at Kent Hall. There were at least a couple dozen people there and it was pretty clear to me that one of the cheerleaders wanted to hook up with me (especially since one of her friends told me she wanted to). She stayed close to me the whole night and was really flirtatious.

As the evening wore on, the pressure built because I knew what I had to do. Finally I said to myself, *Okay, I've got to get this done, so let's do it.* So I took the cheerleader's hand and led her to my room and we were there for maybe thirty or forty-five minutes, which was about thirty or forty-five minutes too long for me. It wasn't like it was the first time I'd ever done this, so I knew what I was supposed to do. And it wasn't the worst thing in the world, but the only reason I did it was to get people off my back for at least a little while.

Of course that wasn't the end of the constant pressure—from my teammates or from the girls who wanted to hook up with me. And it could be intense. One time I came back to my room and found a girl in my bed waiting for me. And for a while I had a stalker who somehow knew where I was going to be, and she'd just show up at the places I was going. I never figured out how she did it, but she must have had scouts who tracked my movements.

One irony about the timing of my prove-you're-straight hookup was that around the same time I was doing my best to prove I was straight, back at home in California the state legislature had passed a bill legalizing same-sex marriage. It was the first time a state legislature had passed that kind of bill without having its hand forced by the courts. That was so *not* about my life and the life I wanted for myself that I doubt it even registered on my radar.

My knee held up fine through the season, although I had to take care of it and ice it after every practice and game. It wound up being an incredible season for us, which ended in December with the NCAA championship, and which we won for the first time since 1968. Winning that championship is the goal for any college athlete and to do it my freshman year, when I was eighteen, was amazing!

The thing about the NCAA championship is that no one's a professional. You're not playing for money. You're playing for your school and for your teammates. And the win came after a season of being with my team on campus and training together, going on the road together, and competing together. When you win the championship you also get a ring. The ring is the least of it, but it's an enduring reminder that I came out on top at the end of my first season playing for the University of Maryland.

Mom flew out for that championship game, which was against New Mexico. We won 1–0. When I talked to my mother about it recently, she said it was one of those times when she had the uneasy feeling that I was bottled up, that I was hiding something. I don't remember holding back, but here's what she told me:

> I was so excited about being able to be there and to see him reach one of his personal goals and see the Terps take it all. But when I saw him after the game, just before he got on the bus and left, he said, "Great to see you. Glad you came. Bye, Mom." And he got on the bus to go. There was almost no emotion in what he said and it made me think that there was something with Robbie that was compartmentalized. All of the normal, natural outpouring of emotion over winning just wasn't there. I had to wonder why Robbie was so contained when all of his friends were celebrating their victory with each other and their families. It would be years before I had any idea just how much he was keeping inside.

I wasn't yet aware of it then, but the whole gay thing was weighing on me, which made it difficult to really experience the kind of joy that came along with winning a championship. I knew I should have been happier than I was; I could see how excited everyone else was, but I just didn't feel it and I didn't know why.

Most of my time in Maryland I enjoyed myself so much and was so busy with classes and soccer and partying that usually I didn't think about what I was keeping inside. But sometimes I did, and when I thought about it I realized I wanted more than anything else in the world to be like my straight siblings, who could get married and have kids. And somehow I persuaded myself that I was not only capable of doing that—marrying a woman, having kids—but I might even be kind of happy doing it.

As an athlete I was very, very disciplined, so if I put my mind to doing something I could do it. So, I asked myself, why couldn't I marry a woman one day and be happy about it? Of course being disciplined had nothing to do with trying to change your sexual orientation, because that's not something I could change any more easily than a straight guy could if he wanted to become gay. But I was really ignorant about sexuality and the fact that it can't be changed, so I tried.

That's how I wound up getting involved with a girl for the first time beyond a one-time hookup. This happened toward the end of my freshman year. I don't want to overstate what we had by calling it a relationship, but "Leslie" and I would hang out and we hooked up a few times. There was something about Leslie that I thought could change me. Leslie was very pretty, really nice, and when I touched her I enjoyed it—not that I was excited by the experience of touching her, but it was fine.

You would think this would be a straightforward process. All I had to figure out was, did having a sexual relationship with Leslie change me from a man who was sexually attracted to other men to a man who was sexually attracted to women, to Leslie in particular? But what was going on in my head was anything but straightforward.

To understand what kind of mental gymnastics I was going through and why this was such a tortured process, you have to put yourself in the shoes of a nineteen-year-old who really didn't want to be gay and had worked really hard at never being attracted to other guys. I was so good at it that I could even talk to attractive guys I knew were gay and squash any sexual feelings I might have had for them before they could even register. So it wasn't like I was making any effort to get in touch with what I felt in my heart of hearts. Instead, I was trying to convince myself that whatever spark of attraction I had for Leslie might somehow mean that I could have a relationship with a woman and really like it.

What turned out to be really confusing for me was that when Leslie and I were apart, when we were not in the same space physically, I could convince myself that I was actually sexually attracted to her. But when I was with her physically I felt I was gay. Let me see if I can explain this. I could have sex with Leslie, but afterward I couldn't wait to get away from her or to get her to leave my room—it was the same experience I'd had with every other girl I'd had sex with. The difference here was that I really liked Leslie. And while I could manage the sex, which felt okay, I couldn't deal with the intimacy after sex, even with her. I didn't want to cuddle or talk. I just wanted to be alone. I'd try pretending, but I couldn't fake feeling intimate, and that's what forced me to face the truth. I was gay and no girl, not even Leslie, could inspire the kind of desire I instinctively knew had to be there if I was going to have a relationship with a girl. It just wasn't there. And I knew instinctively it would be there with a man, if I liked him in the way I liked Leslie.

You would think that from that point forward I would have simply accepted that I was gay and whether I liked it or not I was going to be gay for the rest of my life. But I wasn't yet done trying, because maybe there was another girl out there who would somehow inspire the change I so desperately wanted. Because I still thought I'd have to figure out a way to get married to a woman and have kids so I could play professional soccer and avoid being rejected by my family. Being gay and open about it wasn't an option. And I couldn't imagine being like one of those guys I'd heard about growing up who was secretly gay, but married to a woman. I wanted to *want* to marry a woman without being secretly gay and sneaking around having sex with men outside of the marriage.

In retrospect it seems silly that I'd ever thought that dating a woman could make me straight or that I had any hope of managing to pull off a heterosexual marriage, but I was young and really ignorant. I know there are books out there that could have helped me understand myself, but I would never have risked being caught reading them or even searching for information online.

After freshman year, Leslie and I talked occasionally and sometimes I'd see her, but we never hooked up again. But despite what should have been a critical turning point in my thinking about my sexuality, I wasn't yet ready to give up on my hope that the right woman could somehow change me.

On balance, I loved my first year at the University of Maryland, my teammates, my coach, and my friends. And the fact that I'd had the best year of my life on the soccer field to date and helped my team win the NCAA championship definitely helped balance my struggles over being gay and wanting to be straight. Leaving aside what happened with Leslie, I truly had never been happier.

So during the summer after my freshman year, when I was offered the opportunity to turn professional and play for a team in the Netherlands, you might have thought I'd seriously think about what I'd be giving up. I remember telling a reporter at the time that it was going to be a difficult decision because "I love college and I enjoy my team and friends . . ." but the truth is it wasn't a difficult decision and once I made it I never looked back. And that makes me wonder if there was something going on subconsciously for me. Maybe I wasn't as happy as I told myself I was. Maybe I was looking for a way to get away, especially after that disappointing experience with Leslie. Maybe I was looking for a way to put even more distance between me and my family.

Now, with an offer on the table to play professional soccer in the Netherlands, I had an opportunity to get away from all that, from the questions from my teammates about girlfriends, from the girls I knew weren't going to be the answer to my prayers, from my family and their natural curiosity about my love life. (My sister Alicia came to visit me in Maryland one time and tried to get me drunk so I'd answer her questions about whether I had a girlfriend or had ever had a girlfriend.) Moving to the Netherlands meant I could get away from all that and get a fresh start in a place where no one really knew me. And, not incidentally, I'd get to fulfill a childhood dream of playing professional soccer in a part of the world where soccer is king.

Whatever was going through my mind at the time, consciously or subconsciously, there's one thing that I'm certain never occurred to me about leaving my life behind at the University of Maryland and moving to Holland. It never crossed my mind that things could get a lot worse.

CHAPTER 7

A DREAM COME TRUE?

If my mother had been making the decisions for me, I would have had a second year in Maryland, as well as a third and fourth. And if *I* were my mother that's exactly what I would have wanted for my son, as well. My mother was old enough to have had the long view, to know that soccer wouldn't always be a part of my life, that professional athletes have a short half-life and I'd have a lot of life to live once my soccer career was over. But try telling that to a nineteen-year-old boy who is having to make a choice between going back to play college soccer for another year or signing a very lucrative contract with a professional soccer team in Europe. (I don't recall the money being a draw for me, but I can't imagine that a six-figure salary that increased to nearly a half million dollars over five years didn't impress me.)

My whole life I'd told myself I wanted to be a professional soccer player before I turned twenty, so my mother never stood a chance against the forces that were pulling me across the ocean and the people who were encouraging me to go. And that included my father, who took on the task of negotiating my contract. In fact, I didn't even bother to include my mother in the discussions until the last minute, because I knew she'd be against it and I didn't want to hear it. Looking back now, I can see that shutting out what I didn't want to hear was something of a pattern for me. And that's what I did to my mom.

Just as I never seriously considered how much I'd miss my friends, my teammates, and my coach in Maryland, I didn't stop for a second to think about what it would be like to live in a rural part of the Netherlands where the weather was guaranteed to be awful. I might also have tried to imagine what it would be like to live in a small town where I didn't speak the language. But I didn't consider any of that. I've always been focused on going forward, forward, forward, and I've done that at my own peril.

At the start of the summer following my freshman year I had no idea that by summer's end I'd be on my way to the Netherlands. I was still thinking I'd stay at Maryland for at least two years, which was what I'd told Sasho, my coach. But even before the summer I'd been getting calls from sports agents letting me know that there was interest from soccer clubs in Germany, Holland, and the UK. I knew enough to know that "interest" didn't mean much, especially since in the past no one had come to me with actual offers.

With my first year at college behind me, I went back to California for two weeks and then returned to Maryland to do a summer class in science and to train with my team. I was also scheduled to spend time in Canada training with the U-20 national team in advance of the Milk Cup competition in Ireland, which is an annual youth soccer tournament. Not a typical summer for the average college freshman, but for me it seemed pretty normal.

Before we left for Canada I got a call from a soccer agent who used to come to my Blue Star trainings and who had a connection with SC Heerenveen, the Dutch club I'd played with briefly when I was younger. He asked if I was interested in going back to Heerenveen, just to train. I wasn't stupid and figured they were scouting me, but no one ever said anything, and whether they were seriously interested in me or not I was happy to go. I was looking forward to testing myself against the Dutch players to see how my skills stacked up by comparison. It's no secret that U.S. soccer had a long way to go to meet the standards of the rest of the world.

I went for ten days and it was a lot of fun. SC Heerenveen is an amazing club with a great system for building young players. The facilities were awesome and the people there were really friendly. The town itself is simple and . . . well, boring. About forty-three thousand people live there, but it's quiet and there's not much to do outside of playing soccer.

So then it was back to Maryland for a few days before going to Toronto, Canada, to train with the U-20 national team before we all headed to Northern Ireland. I didn't know it, but SC Heerenveen sent scouts to the Milk Cup to watch me play and fortunately I played really well. In an online article that I read later, a reporter who was there said that the Dutch scout watched me score the goal of the tournament, "volleying a ball over a defender and then striking it on the fly, sending a laser beam into the back of the net to cement the good impression he had made on the training ground in Holland."

After the tournament, my national team coach got a call from a representative from Heerenveen telling him to let me know they wanted me to move to Holland to play for their team. I loved the idea because it was a great club and I liked the players and coaches I'd just met. At that point I brought my dad into the conversation so he could deal with the contract negotiations, and then I headed back to Maryland to talk to my coach, pack my stuff, and return to Holland.

By now I'd told my mom what was going on and she insisted on meeting me in Maryland and also insisted on paying for my flight from Holland back to the United States. (My mother had paid previously for all of my travel to play with professional teams in the Netherlands so I could maintain my amateur status. If I'd allowed any of the professional teams to pay for my travel I would have lost my amateur status and wouldn't have been allowed to play college soccer or play for the U.S. national team.) Mom insisted on paying because she still held out hope that she could persuade me (with Sasho's help) to say no to Heerenveen and return to playing for Maryland. I didn't see any point in arguing with my mother and let her pay for my ticket, but my mind was made up.

When I arrived in Maryland I sat down with my mom and dad and Sasho. I explained to Sasho that I'd had no intention of leaving Maryland, but that "this is an offer that I can't turn down." Sasho asked if I was sure that I didn't want to play for the MLS (Major League Soccer) in the United States instead. By this point MLS said they'd match my contract at Heerenveen. I said, "I don't want to hear what they have to offer because whatever they offer they can't give me the same kind of development and experience that I'll get in Holland." I envisioned going to Holland and working my ass off for a year learning from the best, and then working my way up from Heerenveen's Reserves division to the first team and building a name for myself in Europe. Sasho was disappointed, but he understood. In an interview with socceramerica.com he said, "Although losing Robbie at this point in time is significant for us because of his special qualities as a player and a person, I am extremely happy to see him fulfill his boyhood dream."

At the meeting, my dad said he thought that going to Holland would be a great thing for my development as a soccer player and a huge opportunity. I'd get to learn better technique, train with better players, and play competitive games. I didn't need convincing, so I think my dad was just trying to persuade my mother that it was the right choice for me. My mom could see there was no hope of changing my mind and gave up. I could tell she was really angry with my dad and I'm sure that didn't help with their already tense relationship. But to tell you the truth, I wasn't paying much attention to what was going on between my parents because I was so focused on how excited I was about going back to Holland to be a professional soccer player.

Reality didn't set in until later that week when I started saying my goodbyes. One evening my teammates and I went to a bar and they all gave me hugs and wished me luck and were excited for me. No one else was turning pro from Maryland, and as far as I knew, I was one of the only college freshmen to sign with a foreign club during the off-season.

During that week between signing and leaving, I had the chance to think about what I was leaving behind. I'd just had the best year of my life—we'd won the national championship, I'd made some great friends on the team and at the university, and I was really close to the coaching staff. I didn't have any worries (other than the gay stuff, and I wasn't thinking about that). My college was being paid for. The whole thing was amazing and I loved it. But when I made my decision to sign with Heerenveen, I just thought, *Oh, I have a great offer to play soccer in Europe, that's my dream*. Then, as I got ready to go, I found that I was really sad to be leaving Maryland and moving to a new country.

But the deal was done and I was flying back to Holland whether I was ready or not. So I packed all my stuff into two big Nike duffel bags, got on a plane, and flew to Holland. A member of the Heerenveen staff met me at the airport and he took me to the furnished apartment in Heerenveen's city center where I was going to stay for the next three months, before I found a place of my own. I took my bags into the bedroom and started unpacking. I was excited about getting ready for training the next day, but I was sad, too, because I was already a bit homesick for Maryland, my friends, my dorm, and my teammates. I felt like, *Okay, this is my new life. This is what I wanted, so I'd better figure it out and get used to it.*

The first two weeks were rough because I was waiting for a work permit and without it I couldn't play. (I was allowed to train, but not play in games.) I think I was also in shock, which might explain why my memory of those first couple of weeks isn't really clear. But from a telephone conversation my mom recalls from that time it's clear that I was really struggling and was having major second thoughts about my decision to leave Maryland. Here's what my mom remembers:

He called and said, "I'm so homesick." And then within five or six months he said that he was so miserable he wanted to come home. Remember, Robbie had just signed a multiyear contract, so he couldn't just turn around and say, "I'm going home." So when he first called to say he was homesick, I said, "I'm here for you. We're going to work this out." And this wasn't just one call. Robbie would call frequently and we'd talk for two hours. He'd say, "Mom, please talk to me." It reminded me of when Robbie was a little boy. He'd seen a scary TV movie called *It*, which was a Stephen King miniseries that Robbie should never have watched. But he did and afterwards he came to my room and said, "Please don't let me go to sleep. If I go to sleep, he'll come." So I stayed up with him all night long until he finally crashed. Robbie's calls from the Netherlands reminded me of that. I could tell that he was feeling terribly alone and was scared to death.

Looking back, it makes perfect sense to me that I was in shock and scared and homesick. Whatever problems I was having dealing with my sexuality in Maryland, I'd left a tight-knit and supportive community where I'd felt like I was part of a large family. Then overnight I'd arrived in a place where I didn't speak the language, where the culture was different, where I was just another professional soccer player, and on top of that I was still a fearful and closeted nineteen-year-old.

Thankfully, once the permit came through I was able to play, and just getting into a routine helped take my mind off of being homesick. On a typical day I'd wake up at seven-thirty, have breakfast, and then drive over to the training ground around eight-thirty or nine, which was only five minutes away. Then, as a team—there were thirty of us—we'd spend a half hour together upstairs at the stadium having coffee or tea. After that, we'd all go downstairs and get our training kit and by ten we were on the pitch to train.

Training was different every day, but we'd run and do ball work, like passing, playing with goals, and possession, where you keep the ball away from each other. Sometimes we'd do fitness training, and then we'd finish with shooting at the goal. Then we'd come back to the stadium and have lunch as a team. After lunch we might have a second training session, which would be more technical, where, for example, we'd work with the wingers on crossing balls.

The training really helped me as a soccer player, but it was a challenge getting used to a different style of play, and I was under a lot of pressure to learn quickly because they'd paid a lot of money for me and expected me to learn the ropes and move up to the first team during my first season. The team's coach, Gertjan Verbeek, said as much to a reporter from the website yanks-abroad.com, which covers U.S. soccer players who play for teams around the world. When asked whether they expected me to move up to the first team, he said flatly, "Of course, because otherwise we wouldn't give him a contract. He's an expensive player for this team because he is not a European."

The challenge for me in the Netherlands was never about improving my skills and learning how to play like a professional. I didn't have a problem learning the ropes. In my few games—we had a game once a week at the small stadium for the Reserve team—I scored three goals and loved every minute of play. The problem was the homesickness, which never really went away. And as the weeks passed and the homesickness got worse, I got more and more depressed, and the more depressed I got, the less confidence I had, so by the fourth month it really hurt my ability to play.

The thing about homesickness, as I've come to understand it, is that if you're able to make connections—get to know people, make friends—you're able to establish yourself in a new community and the homesickness fades. In Maryland, I had a built-in community. The soccer team was like its own fraternity, Sasho was a father figure, and the rest of the coaching staff were like big brothers to us.

It was totally different in the Netherlands. I was living on my own, far from friends and family. I didn't speak the language. (I was taking Dutch classes, but it was slow going.) I came from another culture. And the fact that I was gay and closeted made it all the more difficult to have a real relationship with anyone, because it wasn't like I could have an honest emotional conversation with anyone where I talked about how I'd get a cramp in my stomach every time I went into the locker room. The Netherlands is a really liberal place, but my teammates still used the word "fag" and I'd get drawn into conversations where I had to pretend to talk about girls as if I were straight. It wasn't like I was even very good at it, but I thought if I didn't participate my teammates might start to wonder about me.

Everything seemed to conspire against connecting with my teammates. For example, if I'd been comfortable going out to clubs with them I might have gotten to know some of them better. I did it a few times, but it was awful. For one thing, the clubs around Heerenveen were so different from home. They were dark, with flashing lights and techno music, which wasn't for me. But the worst was having to pretend that I was interested in girls. After the first couple of times I never did it again, because I had enough problems without putting myself in a situation where I'd have to flirt.

I wasn't entirely alone, because I became friends with this one Spanish guy on my team, Gonzalo Garcia, who lived across the street from me. Sometimes I'd go to his place and play video games and we'd go out to eat. But usually after training I'd go home and Skype, or be on Facebook, or check email. I'd call my mom, Alicia, or Dad at all hours and we'd talk about what was going on in their lives, but I didn't say much beyond the surface about mine, although it helped just to hear their voices.

I wound up spending a lot of time alone, and for me it was really dangerous to be left on my own with my thoughts. I obsessed about being gay and what that meant for my life. Was I ever going to be able to come out? Was I always going to have this awful feeling in the pit of my stomach? What would I do if I couldn't play soccer anymore? Would I ever be able to have an honest conversation with my family? And why didn't God ever answer my prayers?

It all added up to this giant crazy storm of emotions and

problems that eventually left me feeling like I wanted to stop playing because I was so miserable. I wound up crying a lot and not wanting to leave my apartment. I'd reached the point where I'd get into bed at night and couldn't imagine having to get up one more morning and go into the locker room. And that's when I started thinking it would be easier if I weren't alive anymore. I'd never felt that way before, but I remember driving my car through an intersection and thinking, *What if I drove my car fast through this intersection and I got into an accident and was killed?* But then I worried about what it would mean to be gay and to kill myself. I'm Catholic. Would it be a double whammy in the eyes of God to be gay and kill myself? So I'd lie awake in bed at night and pray out loud: "God, you can take everything away from me, take soccer, I just want to be straight. I would love to be like my brother and sisters."

Even when I was at my most depressed, I didn't think I was seriously suicidal and didn't do anything to endanger my life, but the thoughts alone were scary enough to make me realize that I had to get out of the mess I'd gotten myself into. The question was, how?

Toward the end of 2006 I had three visitors from home—my sister Coco, my Aunt Angel, and my father—and that helped me postpone the inevitable a little longer. The first to come visit was Aunt Angel, my father's sister—my brother, sisters, and I had stayed with her for a month in Orting, Washington, when my parents first separated. I was really close to my aunt, and because she'd always been a really open-minded person I felt comfortable opening up to her a little bit. I confided in her that I wasn't happy in Heerenveen and said, "As much as I love soccer, maybe it's not for me." What I didn't say, what I felt I couldn't say, was "What's got me so depressed is that I'm gay and dealing with these issues. I think that a lot of people in my family won't accept that. And I don't think I could continue playing soccer if anyone had any idea. I'm not sure what I should do. Can you help me figure this out?"

If I'd asked for help I'm sure Aunt Angel would have given it, but I didn't trust her not to tell my dad. I imagined that she'd feel bad for me and would want to help me and that she'd think by telling my parents it might help. So I didn't tell my aunt what was really going on. All I managed to say when she was getting ready to go back to the United States was "Don't leave!"

By the time Coco came to visit a few weeks later in early December, I was really down and couldn't hide it. Mom had sent Nicole "to bring Robbie Christmas" because she couldn't get away herself. She knew I was in trouble and hoped that by sending Nicole it would help. When Coco arrived, she took one look at me and said, "You're legit depressed." I loved having her there, but I didn't even want to leave the apartment. She had to drag me out to go to Amsterdam and, much to my surprise, when I was out of my apartment I actually had a good time.

My father came next, with his new wife, and spent Christmas with me. I didn't know it, but Nicole had told him that I was really unhappy. I love my father and I know he loves me, but when it comes to emotional things we have a "don't ask, don't tell" policy that's sort of like the old U.S. military policy toward gay people that President Obama repealed. My dad repeatedly asked me how I was doing and I would tell him that I was fine, although homesick. I never told him what was really going on for me or that I was thinking of leaving.

For the most part, Dad saw his role as my Heerenveen cheerleader, so I knew he wouldn't want to hear that I was thinking of coming home. He would routinely send me emails that said things like "visualization of positive events is very helpful" and "if a negative thought creeps in switch back to a positive 'kick ass' mind-set." So I knew he wouldn't want to hear that I was thinking of walking away from my big opportunity to play in Europe and coming home.

During my father's ten-day visit we went on long drives and I showed him around northern Holland. We went to Amsterdam a few times and to Groningen. We walked around Heerenveen, went to dinner, hung out, and he came to training sessions. Even though we kept things on the surface and I didn't talk to Dad about what was really bothering me, it was good to have the warmth and comfort I felt just being around him. And of course there were things we could talk about, like soccer, training, learning Dutch, and how people were doing at home.

I can't really blame my dad or Coco or Aunt Angel, or anyone in my family, for not being more understanding and sympathetic, because I kept them in the dark about the fact that I was drowning. As far as they knew I was just really homesick, and it must have been confusing for them that I'd gotten so depressed over that alone. And it wasn't just my family I kept in the dark.

Over time I'd withdrawn deeper and deeper into myself and deeper into the closet, and it would be years before I found my way out.

During my first couple of months in Heerenveen I somehow managed to leave my depression behind whenever I was on the soccer field. Then it got harder and harder to be one person off the field and another on. Anyone watching me play could see that something was wrong. I knew I wasn't playing well, not even close to my standards. I was inconsistent, slow to react, and distracted. So much of how you perform on the field depends on being in a good place in your head. I couldn't get out of my head and it was driving me crazy. I just didn't want to be there, and by February I couldn't take it anymore.

The first person I told was my mother. I knew she would be supportive because she's always been focused on my happiness. I knew my dad would be against it, so I decided to wait to tell him until after I got the ball rolling.

So I called my mother and said, "Mom, I'm so depressed. I can't live here. I need to come back to the States. I don't know what I should do, but I'm miserable." I told her I was miserable because I felt isolated, couldn't communicate with people, didn't have any real solid friends, and wasn't enjoying soccer because of all that. If I could have been honest with my mom I would have explained, "I'm very isolated, mainly because I feel like I can't have a real conversation with people and I can't have a real conversation because I'm gay. And I can't tell people

I'm gay because I don't think they'd understand and I'm afraid they'd never accept me and I'd never be allowed to play professional soccer."

Mom said she wanted me to take a little time to think about what I was giving up. She also asked me what my next steps were and I explained that I'd have to talk with my agent, which I did. I told him that I wasn't at all happy in Europe, that I needed to find a new team back in the States. Then I had to talk with the head coach at Heerenveen, as well as the guy who ran everything, and tell them what was going on. And they said, "We know. We can tell how unhappy you are, because we knew you when you first got here and you smiled, you joked with people, and now you look like a zombie. We want you to be happy here and if you're not happy, we're going to let you go." And they added, "But you have to go back to the States; you can't play for another team in Europe."

I didn't care about playing in Europe. I knew I needed to go back to the States, where I could be around people I could speak with and be closer to my family. I never thought about the fact that I'd still face the same internal issues I had in the Netherlands, because I was still sitting on this huge secret. All I could think about was needing to get out of Heerenveen and going back to the United States and playing for a Major League Soccer team. *That* seemed like the answer.

Once things were pretty much set, I told my dad what I was doing. As I'd expected, he was mad and told me that I was too young to make such a rash decision. He thought I was making a bad choice, that I was passing up a once-in-a-lifetime opportunity to move up to a higher level in my sport, that I was just homesick and would get over it if I tried. I told him I was too depressed to stay, that I was quitting. I didn't give him a chance to argue.

My agent talked to the MLS and they were happy to have me, but it turned out that there was a price to pay for the fact that I'd turned down the MLS to play in Europe in the first place. (When you're coming back from overseas, or sometimes when you're first turning pro, the MLS negotiates your contract instead of the individual team.) I don't know what their exact words were and I don't know who delivered the message, but the message I got through my agent was, "We don't want young players to feel like they can go overseas, and that if it doesn't work out for them, just come back. So we're going to make an example of you." So they offered me a contract for $50,000, which was a really good salary for someone my age, but a huge pay cut from Heerenveen. If they were trying to make this a financially painful decision they really didn't know me, because I didn't really care about the money. Money has never been a motivating factor for me.

Of bigger concern was where I'd wind up playing. That March, MLS put me in a weighted lottery, which meant that the worst teams would have the best chance of getting me and the best teams would have the worst chance. Toronto FC had actually expressed interest in making a deal with Heerenveen to get me, but MLS wasn't about to give me a choice. It was a little more punishment, which made me mad because I wanted to play for a team that actually wanted me and thought that the whole effort to make an example of me was petty. But miraculously it all turned out for the best because the Columbus Crew got my rights (they had a really bad record), and their coach was Sigi Schmid, the coach I'd known since I was eight years old.

Most recently I'd played for Sigi when I was sixteen and had trained briefly with the LA Galaxy—he was their coach at the time. Sigi had been one of the only men who agreed with my mom that I should go to college first before turning pro and going abroad. Sigi could have traded my rights to another team, but he decided to keep me and told me that he expected a lot out of me because he knew what I was capable of and that I'd have the chance to play right away if I did well during the preseason. I'd never felt so lucky in my life and couldn't have been happier or more relieved. And coincidentally, my mother grew up in Columbus and my grandpa went to Ohio State, so in a way I was going home.

Just after I arrived in Columbus, in early April 2007, Marc Connolly interviewed me for ussocerplayers.com and asked me to reflect on my experience in the Netherlands. In reading my words all these years later I can hear that I was feeling insecure and defensive, but determined. Here's what I said: "I learned a lot about life, myself, and the game. I still want to make it. I still want to go to Europe and play, maybe when I'm older. But I know I want to play here where my family and friends can watch me. People might be doubting me or saying that I'm spoiled because I wanted to come back home. So now I just want to prove to people that I'm a good player and, ultimately, a world-class player. I'm going to do whatever I can."

What I didn't say to Marc Connolly, or to anyone, was that as difficult a time as I'd had in Heerenveen—and I wouldn't want anyone else to go through what I had—I was glad for the experience because it made me stronger. I'd lived on my own for the first time, endured terrible loneliness, and found a way out. I was forced to grow up, managing my own money, navigating life in a foreign country, even cooking for myself. And at age nineteen, I still had plenty of time to prove myself, both on and off the field. As shaky as I felt after Heerenveen, I meant every word when I said, "I'm going to do whatever I can" to prove myself. And over the next few years playing for the Columbus Crew I did exactly that.

My mom with three of her seven siblings in 1958. *From left to right:*
Uncle Mark, Mom, Uncle Fred, and Aunt Marcia.

My first birthday at our
house in San Pedro in my
mother's arms, while my
sister Alicia looks on. I
liked cake then and will
always like cake.

We all loved swimming in the pool at my grandparents' house in Rolling Hills Estates. Here I am with my dad in 1989. My sister Alicia is behind me making rabbit ears.

Testing out my first bicycle in the backyard of our house in San Pedro in 1991. I fell in love with Vans (canvas sneakers) at an early age.

Playing in my sister Nicole's room (we all call her Coco) in 1991 with some of our favorite toys (including my toy airplane and my dog—he didn't have a name because I never named my toys).

My cousin Hunter and I were making trouble at my grandparents' house when my mother's youngest sister, Aunt Lisa (we all called her Aunt Lollie), whom we all adored, picked us up and held us tight.

My first grade school picture at Peninsula Montessori. I was clearly a very happy kid.

Running with the ball playing for my first club team, the South Bay Gunners, against the Palos Verdes Crusaders, in the mid-1990s. I was really excited to finally be playing competitive soccer. I was two years younger than most of my teammates, which is why the other players look so much bigger than me.

On the field in Torrance, California. Proud, but feeling shy, holding our State Cup medal in 1994.

Goofing on the sofa at my grandparents' house in the mid-1990s, not long before my parents divorced. *Left to right:* Alicia, Mom, Timmy in a standard Timmy pose, Coco, Dad, and me.

Playing "Cool Girls" at my grandparents' house with my sister Coco. She's dressed up as a ballerina. I'm just some weird creature without a name.

As a purple belt in judo I won the gold medal in the Junior Olympics in 1997. I felt like a champion!

At age twelve, I was playing for the PV Raiders (Palos Verdes Soccer Club) on our home field in Rolling Hills Estates. That's my good friend Steven Lenhart, the squinting blond in the back left corner, playing for the opposing team, Jusa Select.

With my mom's parents (Grammers and Grandpa) and my cousin Matt, freshman year of high school at Mater Dei in 2001. I have no idea what event this was, but we all look very happy.

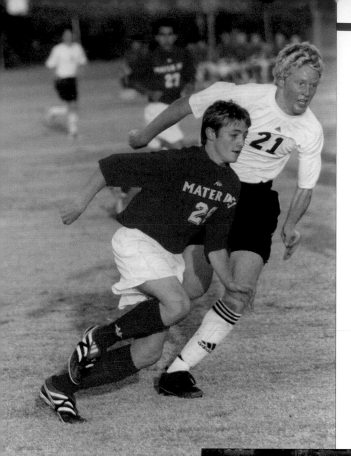

Chasing the ball and enjoying high school soccer my freshman year at Mater Dei. I've always been very competitive, no matter how big or fast my opponent was.

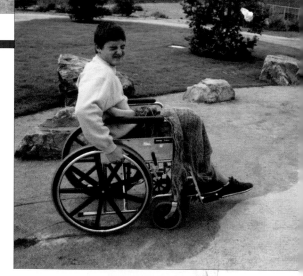

Right after my first knee surgery in the summer of 2002, before starting my junior year at Huntington High School, I was confined to a wheelchair for six weeks. Here I'm joking around with my mom, who took the picture, but I was miserable.

CHAPTER 8

MY CHAMPIONSHIP SEASON

Robbie Rogers is Major League Soccer's most exciting young player. He is also arguably its fastest.

—THE COLUMBUS DISPATCH, MAY 13, 2008

There's no way to describe the sense of relief I experienced when I landed in Ohio to play for the Columbus Crew. I was going to be playing for a coach I knew well and liked, in a place that was familiar to me because of my family, where everyone spoke my language, and to top it off I was invited to live with two former teammates from the U-17 residency in Florida and the U-20 national team, Tim Ward and Danny Szetela. I was also reunited with two of my college teammates, Jason Garey and Marc Burch, who played for the Crew when I got there in 2007.

Tim Ward is a really cool guy from Wisconsin. He's quiet and shy, but funny when you get to know him. Danny Szetela is a very passionate and emotional Polish guy from New Jersey. The house we lived in was Danny's place—a scary old house with weird dark orange carpeting on a large piece of property in

Dublin, an affluent suburb about twenty minutes outside down-town Columbus.

But before going into any more detail about my first five seasons playing for the Columbus Crew, I should first explain—for those who don't follow soccer—how professional soccer is structured in the United States. In brief, U.S. soccer has a Western Conference and an Eastern Conference. There are nine or ten teams in each. If you're on a Western Conference team you play each of the Western Conference teams three times and the Eastern Conference teams at least once. There are thirty players on a team's roster, but only eleven players start in a game (with the exception of my first season with the Crew, I was generally a starter), and another seven players serve as substitutes. At the end of the regular season, whichever team in either conference has scored the most points overall wins the Supporters' Shield.

Over the course of the season you play a total of thirty-six to thirty-eight regular-season games. If you make the playoffs, you play another four to five games. Five teams from each conference make the playoffs. And then the winners of the Western Conference and Eastern Conference compete against each other for the MLS Cup. During the course of the season you may also play four or five international games with teams from abroad. These games are called "friendlies," but they don't count toward a team's record for the playoffs, and while they're "friendly," they're incredibly competitive.

Of the three soccer leagues in the United States, Major League Soccer is the top league. The other two leagues are like the minor leagues in baseball, but, unlike with baseball, all three soccer leagues compete against each other for the Open Cup, a competition whose roots date back about a century.

In Europe and around the world, each country has its own league, and they don't consider America's MLS to be of the same caliber. So you can understand why my father was upset when I bailed out of playing in the Netherlands and signed with the Columbus Crew. But whether or not it was a step back in my career, returning to the United States to play for the Columbus Crew marked the beginning of an amazing time for me, although for virtually the entire five seasons I played for the Crew I wound up living my life on two separate channels. I really didn't see how I had any other choice.

On the public channel, I was Robbie Rogers the up-and-coming professional soccer player who helped his team win the national championship. On the other channel, which virtually no one saw except in glimpses, I was Robbie Rogers the fearful, closeted, struggling young man who couldn't figure out how to deal with the reality of who he was.

Before I get to the Robbie Rogers I kept hidden from public view, I'd like to tell you about my public life as a professional soccer player, because my time with the Crew proved to be some of the most exciting years of my career. Between April 2007 and December 2011, I made 138 appearances and scored seventeen goals (if you don't follow soccer you'll have to take my word for it that this is a very good record, especially for someone as young as I was at the time), helped my team win the MLS Cup, was chosen to play on the All-Star team, made multiple appearances on the U.S. national team, and went to Beijing with the U.S. Olympic soccer team.

It's probably fair to say that the Crew was a pretty crappy team when I joined them at the start of the 2007 season. They hadn't won a playoff series since 2002 and had never won the MLS Cup in their thirteen-year history. But Sigi Schmid is a brilliant coach and he was in the process of building a stronger team, so I was lucky to be there in 2007 to help in that effort and to benefit from Sigi's coaching. Although I spent a lot of that first season watching from the bench and we failed to make the playoffs, I felt a big sense of accomplishment scoring three goals in the ten games I played. (I scored two of those goals in the season's finale against D.C. United.)

There were two high points for me during the 2007 season. The first was my first goal as a U.S. professional soccer player, which came toward the end of the season in a game against New England. Ned Grabavoy played a ball to me over the top, and I ran onto it. I had a one-on-one with the goalie and I passed it with my left foot to the side and that was my first goal. It was just a goal, but I was excited to have achieved that milestone and let myself enjoy the moment.

The other high point came in the middle of the summer when my roommates, Tim and Danny, and I went to the FIFA U-20 World Cup in Canada for a month of training and competitions. (FIFA stands for Fédération Internationale de Football Association, which is the international governing body of association football.) It was a big deal and an amazing coincidence that the three of us went together, because they pick the best American players who play for U.S. teams and for teams around the world to create a single team of about twenty guys to play against the best teams from Brazil, France, Holland, you name it. Twenty-four teams played fifty-two matches. More than a million people came to watch the games, which were played in six cities across Canada. We had a really great showing, but ended up losing in the quarterfinals to Austria.

The 2007 season was just a warm-up for 2008, because that was the year we won the Supporters' Shield and then the championship—we exceeded everyone else's expectations, but not our own. Sigi had brought in some new guys—a combination of promising new talent and well-experienced older players—and he traded away some players who weren't part of his plans. We all got along and we had a good locker room— there weren't any big egos, so it was a very positive environment.

From the start of the 2008 season we were playing well and I was really happy with my game. Although I didn't pay attention to what was being said in the press, I know that my father did. He kept all the newspaper and magazine clippings and printed out reports from online. Shawn Mitchell from the *Columbus Dispatch* called me "the most dangerous American left-side player early in the season." *Soccer America Magazine* put a picture of me on their cover under the headline "MLS Rising Stars." I was named MLS Player of the Week for week seven of the season, right on the heels of David Beckham, who was playing for the LA Galaxy and was the previous Player of the Week. (I'd had two goals the Saturday before in our come-from-behind win over the San Jose Earthquakes—which put us into first place in the Eastern Conference. The MLS Player of the Week is chosen each week of the MLS regular season by a panel of journalists from the North American Soccer Reporters [NASR], which includes members of the print, television, radio, and online media.) I got six goals overall for the season and was an MLS Goal of the Year nominee. I was also named a Best XI, which is an annual award recognizing the league's top eleven players at each individual position on the field: one goalkeeper, three defenders, five midfielders, and two forwards.

In the middle of the 2008 season I got voted onto the "starting XI" MLS All-Star team. The first eleven players are determined by votes from fans, the media, players, and coaches, as well as the general managers. The All-Star coach and the MLS commissioner pick an additional seven players for a total of eighteen, and they also decide who the starters will be. Because 2008 was my first year as a starter for the Columbus Crew, I was in shock when I found out I'd been picked. But I wound up not being able to play because soon after I was named to the U.S. Olympic team and the schedules conflicted. So instead of playing on the All-Star team I wound up going to Beijing. It was all so exciting and happening so fast that I could hardly take it in.

I had some doubts that I'd actually make it onto the Olympic team because I wasn't chosen for the Olympic qualifiers, which take place several months before the actual Olympic team is chosen. This requires some explaining, because the process of putting together the Olympic team isn't exactly straightforward.

Several months before the Olympics I was invited to go to China by the U.S. team's head coach, Peter Nowak, to practice with what effectively was a prequalifying camp for the Olympic team. Getting chosen at that point was no guarantee you'd make it onto the team that played in the actual qualifiers or the final Olympic team itself. The prequalifying camp is more of an opportunity to demonstrate your skills and for the coach to see if you fit in with the kind of team he has in mind. We played a couple of games against the preliminary Chinese Olympic team and when we got back home I wasn't chosen to be on the team to play in the qualifiers. I was really sad about that, but I set my mind on doing the best I could during the regular season with the Crew in the hopes that I might get called up later for the final Olympic team. And that's how things played out.

This is how it was reported in the soccer press at the time. On July 17, 2008, Michael Lewis of MLSnet.com wrote:

> Coach Nowak said of Robbie, who had scored five goals in sixteen games (started in all sixteen) with the Crew, which made him second on the team, "It's no secret that Robbie has [had] a great season . . . and the whole team is playing very well. In the last couple of months, Robbie has started to play the game everybody loved to see him play. He's had a lot of very significant progress in the last six, seven months and this is good to see. He's healthy, he's fit, he's scoring goals and he's helping his team win . . . He fits the picture very well."

A few days later, Andrea Canales, writing for ESPN Soccernet, said:

> No other player on the squad forced his way onto the list more than Robbie Rogers. Dropped from the team during qualifying, Rogers channeled his drive into his MLS

campaign with the Columbus Crew, performing so well that he earned accolades around the league and became the youngest player elected to the All-Star game this year. Of course he won't participate in that game because his efforts succeeded in restoring him to the Olympic Squad instead.

I was thrilled when I got the word, because to compete for your country with Team USA and with all of your fellow athletes from around the world at the Olympics was such an incredible honor. And it was something I'd dreamed of from a very young age, so going to Beijing to compete was a dream come true.

Several days later I joined the other seventeen players (including my former Crew roommate Danny Szetela; my friend and former teammate Sacha Kljestan; and two of my teammates from the Terps, Chris Seitz and Maurice Edu) at Stanford University in Palo Alto, California, for training camp, where we were also fitted for opening ceremony uniforms and given our Olympic equipment. Then we headed to Hong Kong for more training and exhibition games against the Ivory Coast and Cameroon Olympic teams. And from there we headed to Beijing, where we were scheduled to play against Japan in Tianjin on August 7, then the Netherlands—also in Tianjin—on August 10, then in first-round play against Nigeria in Beijing on August 13.

The high point for me was the opening ceremonies, which were the most amazing experience I've ever had. Before we marched into the Olympic stadium, the whole U.S. Olympic team—soccer players, basketball players, everyone—met in an auditorium, where President George W. Bush spoke to us. (I can't remember a word he said.) From there we lined up and headed out to join up with the other athletes from around the world who were in a long line circling the outside of the stadium. Then, as we walked through the tunnel leading into the stadium, we all started chanting, "USA! USA! USA!" And once we came through the tunnel and onto the field everyone in the audience—there were more than ninety thousand spectators, if you can imagine!—started chanting along with us. And with everyone taking pictures there were thousands of flashes going off every second. It was surreal!

So we marched around the track with the other teams from every corner of the globe, with each team holding their national flag high. It was such an incredible range of humanity on the field and in the stands. I looked out into the stadium to see if I could find Mom and Aunt Angel, who had flown over to be with me, but it was hopeless.

Once we finished circling the track we were directed onto the field, where we lined up with our team and watched the opening ceremonies—the lighting of the torch and the whole opening ceremonies show, which was totally over-the-top! Unfortunately, because we were on the field, which was where the show was staged, we couldn't actually see the whole thing, so we watched on the huge video monitors. By that point it was all so overwhelming and I was so dead-tired from the travel and the training and the jet lag that I was ready to get out of there. But even if I'd been able to leave and get into bed, there would have been no way to sleep because I was so filled with excitement and joy and pride over just being in China representing my country.

We went into the competition, which was structured like a tournament, with high hopes of at least making it out of our group and maybe even coming home with a gold medal. Because of how the tournament is structured, every point and every game counts, so it was very exciting (I was a starter for each game), especially playing in front of such huge crowds. But our hopes didn't last long. We beat Japan, tied Holland, and lost to Nigeria, and that was the end of it.

It was really disappointing, and after we lost several of us went out to a bar. I was hanging out with my friends and a bunch of American girls and after more than a few drinks we said we were going back to the hotel to get some food. Our coach didn't want us staying in the Olympic Village because he thought we'd get in trouble, so we were staying at a nearby hotel getting in trouble.

Somehow I ended up alone in my room with one of the girls and we made out for a while on my bed. She had a boyfriend, but I guess she thought making out was okay and I was happy to leave it at that. I don't even know how she wound up my room, but as drunk as I was I know I did it to prove to the guys that I wasn't gay. Of course, that was all in my own head because now the only person keeping a scorecard was me.

The next day we were on our way back to the United States. It was the middle of the season with the Crew, so I had to get back to work.

The Crew had such a good season in 2008 (17-7-6) that we clinched a playoff spot two weeks before any other MLS club. And then in the final against the New York Red Bulls we played before a sellout crowd of twenty-seven thousand—including thousands of fans from Ohio—at the Home Depot Center (now the StubHub Center) in Carson, California. Best of all, my family was in the stands—my mom and dad, brother, sisters, and grandparents—to support me. And they were there to cheer us all on when we beat New York 3–1 to win the MLS Cup. After the game my sisters Coco and Katie came down to the field and hugged me and then I went up into the stands to hug the rest of my family.

Later, in the locker room, we hosed each other down with champagne. I don't remember doing any of the hosing or much of anything from right after the game, but there's a photo of me doing it, so I must have. Nick Green from the *Daily Breeze* newspaper, who was in the locker room, wrote that I had a huge grin plastered across my face as I "munched upon a piece of pepperoni pizza." I apparently said, "It never tasted this good." And, I added, "I don't know if I'll ever have a season this great again."

My doubts were well placed, because while there were still high points to come over my next three seasons with the Crew,

I never had another year like 2008. (I played a total of sixty-nine games in the 2009–2011 seasons and had only four goals. I'd had six goals in 2008 alone.) And after Sigi left in 2009 to coach the Seattle Sounders, the Crew never had another year like 2008. We won the Supporters' Shield in 2009, but in 2009 we were still pretty much the same team that Sigi had built and trained.

After that there were a lot of changes, but toughest for me was how different my new coach, Robert Warzycha, was. Sigi knew how to get the best out of his players. Robert wasn't a bad guy, but he wasn't the right coach for me and for a lot of guys who played for him. Although Sigi was hard on me, he also knew when to give me encouragement. Bobby really knew the game as well as any coach, but he wasn't great at communicating with his players. The end result was that his style of coaching didn't bring out the best in me. It also didn't help that I started the 2009 season trying to play through a hamstring injury, which was really dumb because you need to let these things heal or you wind up making them worse.

Despite having to take time off to recover, I wound up making nine appearances that year with the senior men's national team—and eighteen national team appearances in all during my final years with the Crew, scoring a total of two goals in international competitions. As part of the national team in 2009 I played in my first Gold Cup, which is a big tournament here in the United States. The crowds for these tournaments are huge! When we played against Mexico in New York at Giants Stadium it was a sold-out crowd of sixty thousand people. At Soldier Field in Chicago we played against Honduras and it was another sixty thousand. You can't imagine the sound that a crowd of that size makes when the teams first run onto the field. It's deafening and it gets your heart pumping. Then in 2010 I was named to the thirty-man roster for the World Cup in South Africa. (I wound up being an alternate, which was a big disappointment, but still it was a huge opportunity.) And I was on the Gold Cup roster again in 2011. (Unfortunately, we lost to Mexico in the finals in Los Angeles.)

By 2010 I knew I wanted to get traded to another team. I was ready for something new and I felt that I needed to be in a place where a coach could bring out the best in me. But that's not such an easy thing to orchestrate, especially when you've still got a year left on your contract. My hope was to maybe play for Sigi in Seattle, but my agent wasn't able to make anything happen.

Then the next year there was all-too-public speculation about whether I'd be traded, but as my father told me from having read about it online, the Crew management made clear that they weren't going to trade me to anyone unless they were presented with "a heck of a deal." I found the whole process really upsetting and had to tell my dad to stop telling me about the gossip he was reading on the soccer blogs—and there was plenty of it (although it's the kind of stuff that only soccer insiders cared about). When you read good stuff, you get overconfident, and when you read bad stuff, it feels like it's the end of the world. I tried never to pay attention to any of that and still don't.

What mattered to me was where I'd be heading once my contract expired, especially since I felt like I'd wasted the 2011 season playing for the Crew when I was more than ready to move on. I knew I wasn't performing to the best of my abilities and wasn't improving my skills, but the Crew management seemed determined to keep me until the clock ran out. I still don't know why, because they could have easily traded me for someone they really wanted and who really wanted to play for them.

In the end I had solid offers from Portland and Leeds United (in the UK). And much to my surprise the Crew offered me a contract, too. I thought they had to be kidding! As great a time as I'd had with the Crew in the past, and as much as I knew I would miss my friends from the community where I lived (virtually all of my friends on the team had left by then), I had to get out of there. The only decision left for me was, do I go back to the West Coast to play for Portland or head to England and try for a second time to realize that old dream of playing soccer on the world stage?

Now for the Robbie Rogers behind the headlines, the interviews, and the triumphant photographs. I don't mean to suggest that my years in Columbus were all bad on a personal level, because they weren't. There were plenty of times when I was pretty happy playing for the Crew. For example, when I first arrived in Ohio and moved in with Tim and Danny it turned out to be the perfect place for me after the bruising experience of living on my own in Heerenveen. Tim and Danny were good friends, we had a lot of fun together, and they weren't interested in who I was dating, so I didn't have to lie or anything.

Landing in Columbus was something of a fresh start. It was

exciting to meet new players, see a new stadium and new training grounds, and to experience how things worked with Major League Soccer. It was all so new that everything I was struggling with about my sexuality faded into the background, at least for a time.

My daily life with the Crew was very different from how we did things in Heerenveen. We'd wake up at seven-thirty, eat breakfast at home, go to training around nine, start training at ten, be done by noon or one p.m., and then you had the rest of the day to do whatever you wanted. So I'd hang out with Danny and Tim: we'd go to the gym or to the pool by our house. We often cooked at home and had people over for small parties, or we'd go out to eat together. The three of us were pretty much on the same page at that stage of our lives: we were only nineteen or twenty, playing soccer, and trying to make a name for ourselves. And during the 2007 season we were preparing for the U-20 World Cup. So we'd all work out together to push each other so we could be at our best by the time we left for Canada in midsummer.

The locker room was the one place where I was routinely reminded that I wasn't one of the guys. Like every locker room I'd been in for years now, the words "fag" and "gay" were tossed around like an all-purpose put-down, and as much as I tried to protect myself from feeling wounded every time I heard someone say "that's so gay" or "don't be a fag," it cut deeper into an already raw wound. Those words were sometimes said to me directly, like, "Robbie, don't be so gay," but of course no one knew I was gay, so they weren't using those words to put me down as a gay man. Still, it was like a knife in my gut every time.

My teammates always treated me like one of the guys, but for me it felt like all the relationships were fake—not just superficial, but based on one huge lie. The guys would talk about girls—who they'd hooked up with and who they wanted to hook up with—which was hardly surprising, given that they were all straight. I'd try to stay out of the conversations, but sometimes there was no avoiding it, like when one of my teammates would comment on the fact that I wasn't dating anyone or hooking up and say, "Robbie is so picky." The fact is that I *am* picky, but of course that wasn't why I wasn't hooking up with girls.

Every so often one of the older players would say, "Robbie, I've got a girl who wants to meet you." That was always scary for me and I'd have to keep from panicking. Usually I'd just say, "I'm sorry, I'm dating someone." Or sometimes I'd respond, "Okay, yeah, why don't you introduce me to her." And then I'd find a way to make sure it didn't work out, although sometimes I'd wind up hanging out with the girl or even hook up with one, which happened five or six times over the years I was in Columbus. It wasn't like I'd go looking for girls, but there were always girls around at games and they were aggressive. Sometimes I felt like I had to test myself and see if maybe I'd actually enjoy it, and sometimes I was just afraid to say no because I thought the people around me would start to wonder. Or I'd do it in an effort to demonstrate that I wasn't gay, like that time at the Olympics.

One downside of doing really well on the soccer field was the press attention that went along with it. I was always nervous about the questions, because invariably I'd get a question about whether I had a girlfriend, like the time in 2008 when I was interviewed, along with my roommate Brad Evans and another teammate, Danny O'Rourke. (By then Tim had been traded to Colorado and Danny Szetela was playing for a team in Spain, so I'd moved to downtown Columbus to share an apartment with Brad.) It was a fashion story for *C* magazine. The three of us were featured on the cover and we were interviewed together. One of the questions was: "What about ladies?" Here's how we responded:

BRAD: I've had a girlfriend for three and a half years now.

DANNY: I've had a girlfriend for about three years now. She just moved here and got a teaching job.

BRAD: But Robbie Rogers is a different story! He's just 21!

DANNY: He's the future!

ROBBIE: I am single . . .

BRAD: He is 21, going to the Olympics from Huntington Beach, California. It doesn't get any better than that.

ROBBIE: But I need a girl who is willing to cook, do the laundry and just chill. We have a really nice couch. Oh, and she needs to enjoy sushi.

BRAD: Okay, it's this mammoth couch from Z Gallerie. It's huge! If you sit all the way back, your feet barely reach over it.

DANNY: We were all watching the Euro 2008 semifinal. It was me, these two and our teammate Stefani. I was all into the game and I looked back and all three of them were sleeping on each other!

ROBBIE: That's why I kind of miss college. You know, because life is pretty awesome. You get to go out and meet a bunch of girls.

DANNY: Do you regret that part of leaving early?

ROBBIE: Yeah, for sure. Now I'm just so busy from work and too tired to even do anything.

I remember when I heard that question I thought, *Ugh! Another time I'm going to have to cover this up.* And I was afraid because I wasn't sure I could come up with answers that were convincing. Reading my words all these years later, I get a weird feeling in my stomach. For one thing, I don't think I was all that convincing, but also I feel sorry for my young self and I feel sorry for anyone who has to live like that now. There are a lot of people who have to lie and hide for their whole lives. And at the time I thought I was one of those people who would have to.

It was pretty early on in my time with the Crew when I was forced to recognize that it wasn't normal that I couldn't enjoy anything. Because 2008 was such an extraordinary year I should have been on a constant high, but I wasn't, and the more success I had, the worse I felt. Everyone around me would be excited, and in the moment I was, too, but as soon as I was back in my room I'd feel numb or sad or depressed, and that left me feeling confused. I'd think, *Why can't I be happy?* I mean, deep down I knew why, but I'd feel confused as to why I couldn't get over this stuff. I'd ask myself, *Am I going to have to deal with this my whole life? Will I always have to hide and lie?* And the more success I had, the more I felt like, *Oh, no, I definitely can't come out because if I come out that will be the end of my career and I love soccer so much that I can't quit now.* It never crossed my mind that I could be gay and play soccer. Never. So the better I did, the more trapped I felt, like there was no way out, that this was how my life was always going to be. One thing I didn't have any understanding of at the time was that by squashing my sexual feelings I crippled myself emotionally, so much so that I often couldn't feel much of anything other than sad and depressed.

The worst was when we won the MLS Cup—the contrast between how I was supposed to feel and how I actually felt was unbearable. I thought that winning the championship would bring me happiness, and it didn't—just like I thought that going to Heerenveen would make me happy, but it didn't. Immediately after the game I was happy. But after saying goodbye to my family I went out with a bunch of the guys to Manhattan Beach to grab a beer. It was weird because we'd just won the championship, which was amazing, and I could see how excited my teammates were, but I thought, *Why am I not happy like they are?* I couldn't experience what they were experiencing. It was as if I were living behind a thick glass wall and could see what they were feeling, but I couldn't feel it. For me it was like watching a movie without sound, which made me feel so alone and left me wondering, *If this doesn't make me happy, what will?* I've come to understand since then that keeping such a tight lid on myself because of my sexuality made it impossible to feel the whole range of emotions that people normally feel, and that's really sad.

I'd actually forgotten that I'd told anyone how unhappy I was, but I talked to Alicia recently and she told me that she remembers a phone call from a few days after the championship. Here's what she recalls: "Robbie had this desperate voice that I'd heard when he was in Heerenveen. He said, 'I'm just really depressed. I should be so happy because I just won the MLS Cup. But I'm not leaving the house, I'm not exercising, and I'm eating a lot. I don't know what I'm going to do.' He was just so tortured and in so much pain and as low as you could be. I was very worried."

Of course, I couldn't tell Alicia what was really going on and I'm not even sure I was fully aware of just how deeply affected I was by living the big lie. Part of the problem, just as it had been in Heerenveen, was that as much as I wanted to connect with people, it was tough. I'd wanted to be close to my friends and teammates, just like I wanted to be close with my family, but since I was hiding something so fundamental about myself and trying to pretend to be someone I wasn't, I wound up feeling isolated whether I was around people or not.

As alone as I'd felt during that time, it wasn't like I didn't know what was going on out in the world, and that there were lots of gay people who lived their lives openly. Even in Columbus, Ohio, there was an annual gay pride festival, and in 2010 there was a parade that went right down the street where I was living with my teammates Steve Lenhart and Cornell Thomas, who did the videography for the Crew. (By this time Brad Evans had been traded and I'd moved yet again, this time across town to the Short North neighborhood.) There was a giant group of gay men and women who went by our apartment, so we opened the window and watched as all these people in drag and wild costumes went by. It was an incredible spectacle and Cornell and I were laughing and having a good time and commenting on what we were seeing. It was one of those very rare occasions, maybe even the first time, when I let myself enjoy the moment instead of feeling like I had to pretend to be indifferent to what I was seeing because I was afraid someone might think I was gay. Still, I was aware that Steve was silent while we were watching, and then he said in a tone of voice that was full of disgust, "I can't watch this anymore," and he walked away from the window.

I guess I wasn't surprised by Steve's reaction because he's a really strong Christian and holds very conservative views about homosexuality and gay people. But I still thought it was a bit childish, because he was acting like, "I can't handle this." I remember thinking two things in response to Steve's disgust. First, I thought, *Even if you're homophobic, relax. It's not like watching a bunch of gay people having a good time is going to bring down the wrath of God.* But it also made me feel like if Steve knew I was gay he would probably be disappointed in me. (Since my coming out, Steve has been one of my biggest supporters. I guess we both had a lot to learn and fortunately our friendship has not only survived, but thrived.)

As I thought about Steve's reaction it wound up really upsetting me, so much so that I talked to my mom about it. I'm not sure whether I was subconsciously testing Mom to see what her reaction would be, but I look back now and wonder why I

COMING OUT TO PLAY

took that risk and also wonder what kind of response I was hoping for. Or maybe I just couldn't contain myself and blurted it out during one of our many phone conversations. Here's what my mom remembers:

> Robbie said something about Steven and I asked, "Have you seen him or spoken with him?" I of course knew they were roommates and had become good friends and was asking what I thought was an innocent question. In response Robbie said something like, "I don't like the fact that he's so homophobic" and he went on to tell me about what Steven said when they watched the gay pride parade go by their apartment.
>
> Now, I knew that Steven was a very good man and had a strong spiritual core. I said, "Robbie, I'm aware of a groupthink phenomenon that goes on, where one person may say something that they expect the other person to hear and agree with without necessarily believing any of it themselves." I think it's what was behind what I said about Elton John when Robbie and I were in the car many years ago and I thoughtlessly remarked that Elton John was gay and Robbie recalls that there was disapproval in my voice. Based on my own personal experience with this sort of thinking I said, "Robbie, be careful what you do with that. Steven has a religious orientation where he may express things in a negative or canned way, and I believe Steven would surprise you if he was dealing with a gay man, person to person."
>
> I think back now and wonder whether Robbie was testing me, looking for me to say, "That's horrible! Why

104

do you think he's homophobic?" And yet, given our relationship at the time I never felt that Robbie was looking for an opportunity to discuss it.

Thinking back, I can see that talking to my mom about Steve was just one slight crack in the armor that I'd built up around myself to keep my secret and to keep myself from feeling my normal sexual feelings. But it wasn't the only crack. It seems silly now to talk about this because I was so terrified back then that anyone would find out what I was doing, but while I was in Columbus I watched two movies with gay themes that were very much in the news: *Brokeback Mountain*, which was about two gay men in Wyoming who carried on a secret, but ultimately impossible, relationship; and Tom Ford's *A Single Man*, which is my absolute favorite movie on so many levels, is about a gay man who finally finds love, only to lose it and his life.

Watching *A Single Man* alone in my apartment made me so sad, because it made me wonder if my only options were to have a fake relationship with a woman or to spend the rest of my life all alone. I thought, *Will I ever be able to love someone the way the main character in that film loved another man? Could I ever have a loving relationship like that?* As sad as I felt, it also left me with the slightest bit of hope that maybe one day I'd meet someone somewhere that I could love and who could love me in return. But as crazy as it may sound, I still wasn't done trying to change—to "go straight."

Toward the end of my time in Columbus, I made one last attempt at having a relationship with a woman. Her name was Katie. She lived in California and traveled a lot for work—she was a model—so we didn't get to see each other often, which in a lot of ways made it easier because there was less pressure on me than there would have been if we saw each other every day.

Katie was so beautiful and we were so similar in terms of our personalities that I thought if anyone could change me it was Katie. (At this point you might be wondering how I could possibly have still been thinking that a girl could change me, but you'd be surprised at what a state of denial I was in, how stubbornly ignorant I was about these things, and how desperately I wanted to change—and don't forget that I was still pretty young.)

When I was back in California to visit my family, Katie and I would go out to eat and talk. When I was in Columbus and we were apart, we'd text. One time she came to a game when we were playing against the LA Galaxy and met my mom in the stands. (I can see why my mom might have thought my relationship with Katie was evidence that I wasn't gay, but that wasn't why I was trying to have a relationship with Katie—it was about my wish to be straight, not an attempt to mislead anyone, at least not consciously.)

Over time I was forced to realize that there was only one problem in my relationship with Katie—and that was me. As much as I loved Katie, I just didn't have any sexual feelings for her. I loved her as a person, I admired her, I could see that she was objectively beautiful, but there wasn't even the slightest spark of sexual energy, at least not for me. And the truth is, beyond maybe making out once, we never had sex. And I'm glad we didn't, because by then I was old enough to realize that I would have been using Katie, and that would have been wrong. I remember thinking about what it would have been like for Katie if I'd been able to pretend I was sexually attracted to her and started an intimate relationship with her. That would have been so unfair to her because I thought she deserved to be in a relationship with someone who could love her in the ways she deserved. As a gay man—which my failed relationship with Katie had finally forced me to finally accept I was—the best I could do was pretend, and what kind of life would that have been for Katie? Or me?

After Katie I never tried dating another woman and never hooked up with a woman again. I knew that if Katie couldn't change me, then no woman could. In a way that realization was liberating because I could finally give up trying. But it was also crushing because I began to realize that sooner or later I was going to have to make a choice—my life or soccer.

CHAPTER 9

THE BIG LEAGUES

I couldn't *not* accept the offer from Leeds United. I'd always wanted to play in the UK, ever since I'd first fallen in love with Arsenal as a child. And given the half-life of a professional athlete—especially one with a balky knee—I figured this was my last chance to realize my lifelong dream. And, not incidentally, it was also an opportunity to redeem myself after my disappointing experience in Heerenveen. But I'd be lying if I didn't admit that part of what went into my calculations—mostly subconsciously—was my wish to go someplace where no one knew me and where I'd be far from my family. This was obviously becoming a pattern for me, but I couldn't yet see it and if you'd asked me point-blank at the time if that's what I was doing, I would have in all honesty denied it.

Here's what was behind my thinking: By going someplace where no one knew me, I wouldn't have to explain to anyone why

I never had a girlfriend. With my family, it was impossible to start with a clean slate, but if I lived in England, it would be easier to keep my secret. We'd only speak occasionally, so they wouldn't know my daily life. And when we spoke it would be limited to Skype calls, which is a lot different from sitting across the kitchen table from my mother. On an occasional Skype call it's hard to really experience a person's full range of emotions, and generally I found it easier to keep those conversations to basic things. If I were facing my mother in person instead of on my computer screen she'd really be able to read my emotions and would want to know more details about what was going on in my life.

For example, when I was home for Christmas, while I was deciding between Portland and Leeds, I was having a conversation with Alicia and she asked me if I'd ever been in love. Face-to-face I felt I had to answer honestly and said that I hadn't been. In response she said, "You deserve love." I managed to switch topics because I didn't want to talk about why I'd never been in love, but then Alicia was telling me about one of her patients who was a lesbian and wanted to marry her partner, and she started telling me how she didn't believe in gay marriage and wasn't sure whether being gay was something you were born with or was learned behavior.

I knew Alicia loved me, but that conversation made me want to run away. And as much as I loved Alicia and the rest of my family, I thought it would be easier if I lived far from them. That may sound counterintuitive given how important my family is to me, but I was just trying to preserve a relationship with them when I was still thinking that if I came out to them, they'd put even more distance between us than the fifty-three hundred miles from Leeds to L.A.

Playing for Leeds wasn't my ultimate dream. Although they had a storied history and were once one of the top teams in the world, by the time they recruited me they were playing in the Championship League, which is one tier below Europe's top league, the Premier League. My hope was that if I went to Leeds and did well I could move to an even bigger club. I wasn't fooling myself that it would be easy, but I was never afraid of working hard and was determined to prove I could do it. Of course I hadn't forgotten my time in Heerenveen, but whenever even the slightest doubt crept in I told myself that I was a lot older, had traveled a lot, and had lived on my own in Columbus. I knew I wouldn't get homesick this time, which I didn't. And as far as what it would be like for a closeted gay man to step into the hyper-masculine world of UK soccer, well, I chose not to think about that and focused instead on the positive, and on my first visit to Leeds I wasn't disappointed.

I was already in Europe playing for the U.S. national team when the offer came in, so I made a side trip to meet with the people at Leeds and check out the team. I flew into Manchester and was picked up by a driver who took me directly to the Elland Road Stadium, where there was a game being played that night. (Elland Road is more than a hundred years old!) I first went to meet with the coach, Simon Grayson, and his assistant, who welcomed me to Leeds and told me they hoped I enjoyed watching the game.

It's hard to describe what it's like to be at a professional soccer game in England if you've never been, because it's such a physical experience sitting in the stands and feeling the energy of the crowd. It's like a single organism made up of thousands of individual fans, a majority of them men. Well, maybe two organisms. There are the local fans, who fill most of the seats in the stadium, and then there are the few hundred or few thousand fans, depending on the game, who have traveled from near or far to support the visiting team. The visiting fans are in their own section, which is cordoned off from the rest of the stadium and surrounded by security people to keep things from getting out of hand—these are very serious fans.

During the game the Leeds fans and the visiting fans choose their chants from their own menu of chants depending upon the play. For example, if a referee makes a call the Leeds fans don't like, they chant, "Shit refs! Shit refs! We only get shit refs!" Or if they're happy with something that's just happened on the pitch, they'll chant, "Stand up as you sing for Leeds!" And when the opposing goalie gets a kick, the crowd chants, "You shit bastard! Ha! Ha! Ha!" However spontaneous it might seem, these chants aren't thought up in the moment. Fans meet routinely in pubs to come up with new chants. For example, when Brian McDermott, who has a shaved head, became manager for one of the opposing teams, the fans came up with: "He looks like an egg. He looks like an egg. Brian McDermott, he looks like an egg." It's a bit obvious, but it really got the crowd going.

Besides the chants, the fans have other ways of letting you know how they're feeling. If the ref makes a call they don't like, they let out a deep, long, rumbling "Booooo" that's so deep and rumbling, it vibrates in your chest. And when there's a goal, the fans explode! They're all on their feet applauding and singing "Marching On Together," which is the Leeds United anthem. (It's played at the start of every game at a brain-rattling volume.) It's not Sondheim, but it's got a catchy, upbeat tune. Here's how it goes:

Here we go with Leeds United,
We're gonna give the boys a hand,
Stand up and sing for Leeds United,
They are the greatest in the land.

Everyday, we're all gonna say,
We love you Leeds! Leeds! Leeds!
Everywhere, we're gonna be there,
We love you Leeds! Leeds! Leeds!

Marching on together!
We're gonna see you win
We are so proud,
We shout it out loud,
We love you Leeds! Leeds! Leeds!

We've been through it all together,
And we've had our ups and downs.
We're gonna stay with you forever,
At least until the world stops going round.

Everyday, we're all gonna' say
We love you Leeds! Leeds! Leeds!
Everywhere, we're gonna' be there,
We love you Leeds! Leeds! Leeds!

Marching on together!
We're gonna see you win.
We are so proud,
We shout it out loud.
We love you Leeds! Leeds! Leeds!

We are so proud,
We shout it out loud,
We love you Leeds! Leeds! Leeds!

After I signed a contract and moved to Leeds I had a lot of catching up to do with my training because I arrived during what would have been the middle of my MLS off-season. I worked especially hard because when you're an American going to play in another country they want to see what you have, so there was a lot of pressure on me to prove myself.

It was February 18, 2012, a full month after I started training with my new team, when I was finally put on the game-day roster and had the chance to play. Coincidentally, that was the same day that the new head coach, Neil Warnock, came down to the locker room to introduce himself. There's always upheaval for a team when a new coach is hired because every coach has his own way of doing things and chooses which players to play (and which players to keep and which to let go) based on his own preferences. But I wasn't thinking about that as I got ready to sit on the bench for the first time. I was just hoping to get called in at some point during the game as a substitute. And then seventy-nine minutes into the game I got the call. Of course, I had no idea when I ran out onto the pitch, my heart pounding with excitement, that after my first eleven minutes of play I'd be on the ground, unconscious, and surrounded by a team of very concerned officials.

I was maybe out cold for a minute or two and then the head physical therapist or the trainer woke me up—my memory is very fuzzy about all of this—and he was looking down at me. They asked me a few questions, checked me over, and then strapped me onto a stretcher (more of a board than a stretcher, to keep me immobilized). Then, as they carried me off the field, the head physio (which is what they call the physical therapists in the UK), Harvey Sharman, leaned over to me and said, "Give the fans a thumbs-up to let them know you're okay." So I gave them a thumbs-up and I could hear people cheer and then applaud. With my head strapped in place I couldn't see anything but the sky. After that, as I was carried through the tunnel that leads from the pitch to the service area under the stadium, I passed out again.

I came to in a room I didn't recognize, with a bunch of people around me. I was pretty scared and thought, *Holy shit, what happened?* That's when they told me I'd collided with another player and might have a concussion. I was still out of it and didn't know if I was at the stadium or in a hospital, but I remember thinking, *Oh, my gosh, this is such a dangerous sport. This is so stupid. I could have been killed.* But even as I was talking to myself, the team doctor who was examining me asked me to watch his finger as he moved it from left to right in front of my face, so he could see if my eyes were tracking properly, which they were. He also asked me how I felt and I said that I felt dizzy and out of it, but I wasn't too out of it to ask who'd won the game. We were tied when I got knocked out, but Leeds scored in the ninety-ninth minute of play and won against Doncaster 3–2.

Once it was clear that I was basically okay, they had me taken by ambulance to the Leeds General Infirmary so I could get a scan to make sure I didn't have a fractured skull or a hemorrhage or some other injury. The assistant physio, Paul Perkins, came with me in the ambulance, and the head physio met us at the hospital. The doctor who examined me asked me to tell him what I remembered about what had happened, and all I could recall was going for a header and that was it. I couldn't remember much about the game before that and all I remembered from after the header was waking up in the room under the stadium. Other than that my memory was wiped, which really scared me. Still, I felt lucky because I knew it could have been a lot worse.

I didn't know until later that my mother had been following the game on the Leeds website, where they have someone reporting the game as it happens. So suddenly she's reading: "Rogers is in. Rogers goes up for a ball." And then: "Rogers is planted on the field. He's not moving. Rogers is being carried off the field." She was understandably frantic and had no way to reach me other than on my cell phone, which I obviously wasn't able to answer. It turned out that she texted a friend of mine to see if he knew anyone who knew anyone at Leeds United, and she somehow got to the assistant physio who was with me at the hospital and he handed me the telephone. This is yet one more example of how fiercely protective my mother is of her five "chickies," as she calls us.

I was instructed by the doctor at the hospital not to train for a week, but even though I was still feeling off the next day, I went to the training ground and met with the physio, who said I shouldn't do anything for at least a few days. So three days later I got on the bike for the first time, which turned out to be a mistake because I got dizzy, sweaty, and nauseous after about thirty seconds of very slow pedaling. I tried again a couple of days later and the same thing happened, so I wound up not doing anything for two weeks.

During my enforced downtime I really came to respect concussions. Until it happens to you, it's hard to imagine how serious it is when your brain gets bruised. I didn't know much about concussions before I had one myself. From my experience they were relatively rare in soccer—maybe three or four a year on my team when I was playing for the Crew. And you never saw someone knocked out cold like I was—at least I'd never seen it before in all my years of playing soccer.

For the first couple of days after I began training again I was nervous about getting hit, but I didn't let that stop me. I didn't let yet another hamstring tear stop me, either—although it set me back more than a week—and within a relatively short amount of time I got subbed into a few games and played some reserve games, just to get fit. Then, on April 14, nearly two months after my concussion, in a game against Peterborough United, I finally made my debut as a starter. I'd had a great week of training, so I wasn't surprised to see my name on the game-day roster, but the real surprise came when one of my teammates said, "You'll probably start tomorrow." I said, "No, probably not. I haven't started before, so why would I now?"

Getting chosen to start means the coach has faith in you, that out of the twenty-five members of your team, you're one of the best eleven guys playing at that moment. It's what all the players strive for. The guys who routinely start every game know in advance that they'll likely be on the list, but I had no clue.

The next day I went to the stadium, and sure enough, there was my name and number on the board in the locker room. I was very excited to have my first start. I'd worked my ass off to get this opportunity and I felt ready.

Just before the ref blew the whistle to start the game, I was standing in the field's center circle by myself and very consciously looked around me to take it all in—just like I did at the Olympics—to appreciate how cool it was to be there and to have this chance of a lifetime. There were nearly twenty thousand people in the stands and the fact that it was a rainy day didn't dampen their excitement; you could feel it crackling in the air. Then the whistle blew and the fans roared to life. We started really well—we were aggressive, we kept the ball, and our team had a few good chances to score. You want the opposing team to be on the defensive, and they were.

About twelve minutes into the game the other team had the ball and one of their players was dribbling around the half-line toward our goal. I wanted to end the play to slow things down, so I chased him with the intention of tackling him and getting the ref to call a foul. That's not something you do every time, but it's one tactic to stop the ball, which gives everyone on your team the opportunity to get behind it. So I tackled him a little bit and fell down with him, and sure enough the ref called a foul.

As soon as I went down I felt like I'd sprained my ankle and thought, *Oh, shit. Debut, I get a concussion. My first start, I sprain my ankle.* But I told myself that I'd be fine, that I'd get up and continue to play. So I tried jogging it off for ten seconds, but this was a really bad sprain—on a one-to-ten pain scale, this was an eight. There was no way I could finish the game, and when I limped off the field the fans stood to applaud. The coach was very kind and said, "You had a great start and it's just really unlucky to have another injury." In that moment I felt more cursed than unlucky.

It turned out to be a lot worse than just a sprain. I was still on the MRI bed when the technician came in and said, "Don't get up. You have a fracture, and if you put any weight on it you could snap the bone." I was shocked and sad and disappointed, because this meant I was done for the season.

By coincidence one of my oldest and best friends, Will Johnson, was coming to stay with me right when I had to go for surgery to have a pin inserted into my ankle to hold everything together. I'm a partner with Will and his dad in Halsey, our menswear business that we launched in 2011. We'd planned Will's visit so we could spend some time in London to meet with a few public relations reps to see if we wanted to expand to the UK. We still wound up going to London, but only for a couple of days, and I was in a cast and on crutches the whole time.

I had to be in a cast for a total of ten days before graduating to a boot. It was an awful experience because I'm a little claustrophobic when there's any restriction on my legs, so having the cast on made it almost impossible to sleep. On top of that I had to give myself a daily injection in my belly to keep from getting a clot in my leg. I'd never done that before and by the end of the ten days, when I flew home for my sister Alicia's wedding, I had bruises all over my stomach.

While I was home I decided to call Armando Rivas, who is

the head athletic trainer at the LA Galaxy, to see if I could do my rehab with them so I could be at home during my recovery. And when the LA Galaxy said yes, I asked my Leeds coach if I could do it and he said, "As long as you come back and you're fit, it's fine with us. We're putting a lot of trust in you. Come back one hundred percent healthy, or it's your butt." I've always taken my training very seriously and so spent May and June working hard and getting my ankle strong so I could go back to Leeds really fit, as promised.

Once I was home and settled into a rehab and training routine, I had the chance to reflect on my time in Leeds, my life in general, and where I was headed. Nothing about my experience in the UK even closely resembled what I'd hoped for, and it made me wonder about my future in soccer. For one thing, it felt like my body was trying to tell me something. It wasn't like the concussion and the broken ankle were my first injuries. I'd had multiple hamstring tears over the years and major trouble with my left knee since I was a teenager. By the time I got to Leeds I'd already had three knee surgeries, including one in 2011 to remove a cyst—that surgery kept me out of play for more than two months. I'd gotten used to babying my knee by icing it and doing lots of stretching and strengthening, but how much longer could I keep abusing it? And the problem with a chronically inflamed knee is that you can't always train properly, which means you can't always do the training you need to get ready for a game.

It's frustrating having so many injuries, but I've had to accept that this is my path, this is who I am, there's nothing I can do to change the body God gave me, so you do the best with what you have and that's it. But after the concussion and now facing a long rehabilitation for my ankle, I wondered how much longer I could keep pushing myself. I was twenty-five and worried (and still worry) that I'd wind up crippled because I played soccer for too long.

Besides the injuries, I had the chance to think about my experience at Leeds as a closeted gay man. I went in thinking it would be easier going to play for Leeds because I'd have a clean slate, but the old locker room issues came up all over again. The only reason I was surprised was because I was so excited about getting to play soccer in the UK that I didn't give myself room to consider what it would be like to play soccer in a place that's long been notorious for its racism and homophobia.

The stuff that went on in the locker room was pretty familiar, but in comparison to my experience with the Crew, walking into the Leeds locker room was like diving into a shoe-box-sized space filled with testosterone-charged gladiators. The thing you have to know about soccer in the UK is that it's a super-macho subculture. You can't begin to compare it to soccer in the United States, where it's much more low-key.

Every day in the locker room was different, but on a typical day you'd go in and everyone says hi to each other and then they start to banter about what you're wearing and who drives what car before moving on to joking about the girl they saw you with the night before, or they'd talk about the girls they hooked up with at a club. And they're always trying to one-up each other—who got the prettiest girl, who slept with more girls, who has the prettiest wife. Everyone's constantly messing with everyone else.

My new teammates were definitely welcoming of me and seemed eager to include me in the banter, although I did my best to stay out of it, especially when the topic turned to girls. Sometimes I had no choice but to say something, although whatever I said was mostly lame and almost always a lie. For example, the guys would often talk about how beautiful the girls are in Los Angeles (they knew I'd grown up there) and I'd force myself to agree. I'd say, "Yeah, the girls in L.A. *are* beautiful and I've hooked up with some of them," which was true. But after a while pretending to be straight got to me, so I mostly wound up saying, "Yeah, they're beautiful," and offered to hook them up with some of the L.A. girls I knew.

If I were straight, the banter would probably have just rolled off my back, but I'm not straight, and what the guys said and how they went at each other left me feeling totally alienated. And it wasn't like I didn't understand that the locker room banter was a way the guys bonded. It's a sort of ritual, almost a game, but it was a game I got worse at over time, and that inability to bond always hurt my game on the field.

Like every other locker room I'd been in, there were way more homophobic remarks than I could count. My teammates would throw around the word "faggot" like it was an all-purpose put-down. I don't think they meant to be hurtful to any particular person or even really believed some of the negative things they said. It was all terribly ignorant, but I could never say anything to counter what I'd heard. I just had to swallow it and keep my mouth shut.

Every once in a while, because gay issues were often in the

news, including gay people in sports, I'd get to hear conversations that made me angry. I remember one time hearing some of the guys talking about the possibility of openly gay players and they said things like, "If gay footballers can shower with us, I want to shower with girls." If I'd had the courage I would have said, "Dude, you have no idea what you're talking about."

Another time, while we were at lunch one day, there happened to be a news story on television about homophobia in soccer, and they talked about Justin Fashanu, who was the first openly gay man to play soccer in England. He was also the first £1 million black footballer. That inspired a conversation (which I stayed out of) about how "there'll never be any more gay footballers." I sat there thinking, *Well, there's one gay footballer I know of sitting in the same room with you, but not any out ones. And given what it's like here, there won't be for a long time.*

I'd never heard of Justin Fashanu before, so after I went back to my apartment I researched him online and read about how there had been rumors about him being gay years before he came out publicly in 1990. And the reaction was horrible. He was a really good footballer, but that didn't matter. He was teased by his teammates, rejected by his own brother, and abused by the crowds—both because he was black and gay. He had a really troubled life after that and wound up killing himself in 1998 when he was thirty-seven years old. Learning about Justin made me so sad and just confirmed for me that if I ever came out, it wouldn't be while I was still playing soccer.

What shocked me most about the anti-gay stuff I encountered in England was what came from the fans. The UK fans are incredibly tribal. They'd kill for their team, which is good *and* bad (and when the UK national team plays other national teams, they'd kill for their national team, as well). One of the craziest examples of that was when we were at an away game against Millwall. I was warming up on the touchline with an-other sub, Mikael Forssell, who was like the David Beckham of Finland. There was a Millwall fan in the stands right near us, who was also Finnish, and he started screaming at my friend in Finnish and calling him every name under the sun, including "fucking faggot!" The guy looked like he wanted to kill Mika, and he did it right in front of his young son, who was standing next to him.

In general, fans in the UK would say whatever awful thing they could think of to try to intimidate the opposing team. I loved the tradition and history and passion around football in Great Britain, but I could never understand why a packed sta-dium in Leeds would chant homophobic slurs when the team from Brighton came to town. It felt like when the pack mental-ity took over, all humanity flew out the door. It was nothing for fans to boo an opposing team and yell "faggot" this and "faggot" that. At away games, when the fans screamed, "faggot" at us I knew they weren't speaking directly to me, so it didn't much bother me because they didn't know I was gay. And even if they'd known I was gay I'm not sure it would have bothered me to have fans from an opposing team curse me.

What scared me was what it would feel like if the Leeds fans turned on me. I saw that happen one time to one of our goalies who had let the ball get past him at a critical moment in a game. The fans went crazy. They were so furious and dis-ruptive that our coach pulled him from the game because he was worried the fans were being so hard on him that it would affect his play, and the team's as well. So whenever I thought about what it would be like to play for Leeds if they knew I was gay, I'd think of that and I couldn't imagine that I could take it. It really scared me to think what they'd say—or do—if they ever found out.

I'm not saying that there weren't attempts by the management to tamp down the anti-gay rhetoric, because there were. For example, at Elland Road there are signs posted throughout the public areas of the stadium asking fans to "refrain from using abusive language" and stating management's "zero tolerance" for "racial, homophobic, or discriminatory abuse." But it wasn't nearly enough, because sometimes it felt like football was so far behind where the rest of society had progressed in its views about gay people and homophobia that it was still living in the Stone Age.

So given my experience in the UK I knew that there was no way I'd ever come out if I was still playing soccer, but while I had every intention of returning to Leeds at the start of preseason, I was still uncertain about the way forward with my life. And that led me to have a lot of conversations with God, because I couldn't imagine continuing to live a life that was so lonely and sad. These were different from the conversations I'd had with God in the past, which weren't really conversations. I was just praying that God would make me straight because I thought there was something wrong with me and that maybe God made me this way to create a giant obstacle for me to overcome.

Now I'd come to realize that there was no way God would

create me this way just to be so miserable, to never be able to have any real relationships, and to never love anyone. So instead of praying to change, I'd pray, "Lord, I need your help. I don't know why I am this way but help me sort that out. I know there's a path for me. Can you help show me what my path is or what my purpose is?"

I'm not sure what led to my change in thinking. Perhaps it had something to do with my experience with Katie and realizing I couldn't change. I think living in England and seeing that there was a larger world beyond soccer also had something to do with it. When I was young I always feared that if I didn't have soccer I wouldn't have anything, including my family's love and respect. I was at a different place in my life now. So I thought, *If I come out and I don't have soccer and my family is mad at me because I'm gay, I've made enough money to support myself and I can go back to school if I want, and have friends, and have a life.* But I wasn't there yet, because I still had a lot of thinking and praying to do, and if I was going to walk away from soccer I wanted it to be my choice, on my own schedule.

By the time I got back to Leeds on June 30 I was really fit and more than ready for the preseason. We did a lot of training, had matches against other teams, I scored a couple of goals, and I felt great. I had every expectation that after my disappointing first season I'd be given another chance. Unfortunately, the coach, Neil Warnock, had other plans.

Before the regular season got under way, Warnock called

me into his office and essentially let me go. He said, "Robbie, I really like you, I think you're a good player, but I don't know you or how I would use you. So if you want to go on loan somewhere, you can do that." Going on loan meant I'd be free to find another team that would let me play for them.

After the coach who first hired me was fired I knew in the back of my mind that this was always a possibility. Every coach likes to put together his own team and I was someone else's player. I was glad that Warnock was honest with me, and thanked him for that, but I was disappointed because I'd had such a great preseason and had been looking forward to demonstrating the kind of playing I'd only given them glimpses of the season before.

I didn't want to turn around and go back to the United States to play for an MLS team. So my new goal was to find a team to play with in England to prove to people I was still a good soccer player, good enough to get asked to play on the U.S. national team again. Then I remembered that one of the coaches who used to coach in Colorado for an MLS team was coaching for Stevenage in London. Stevenage is a League One team, which is the third tier in the English football league system (one tier below Leeds). My optimistic plan was to play there for a few months, do well, and then move back to Leeds or go to another club. And in the meantime I'd get to live in London, explore the city, and do an internship with Trace Publicity, a fashion PR firm (which I'd arranged over the summer when I was back in Los Angeles—Trace was one of the public relations operations that Will Johnson and I met with when we went to London right after my surgery).

It had always been a dream of mine to live in London, and

after visiting a few times when I was living in Leeds, I was sure of it. I loved the history of the city, all the culture, and the fashion and design. And I liked the density. Leeds has a dense city center, but nothing like London, and I'd never had the chance to live in a big city before. So playing for Stevenage would be the ideal scenario.

Everything happened very fast. My agent spoke to the people at Stevenage, who were happy to have me; I packed a couple of bags; and I moved down to a hotel in London for a couple of weeks while I looked for a furnished apartment to rent. I didn't have a lot of time to look, so I couldn't be picky, but I wound up finding this amazing place, the coolest spot ever, next to a park in an East London neighborhood called Clerkenwell. I didn't know until I moved in, but a lot of designers and architects have studios and offices there.

The building had been a brothel and was redone by an architect who lived in one of the two apartments. My front door was a flight up and it was this big red door that swung open and led into the living room. It was a high-ceilinged two-bedroom, with one and a half baths, a beautiful kitchen, hardwood floors, and radiant heat. (I'd never experienced radiant heat before and it's great at keeping you feeling toasty, especially in a cold and damp climate like London's.) The front looked out on Old Street and the back rooms faced the house's garden.

It took me about two months to get used to taking the Tube and learning what to buy at the grocery, because it's not like you could load up your car with a bunch of stuff. You carried what you bought. I eventually learned to ride a bike everywhere, so that's how I got to know the city.

My typical day in London started early because I left my apartment at eight a.m., so I could get to the Kings Cross train station for the twenty-minute train ride up to Stevenage. We'd train until noon and then we'd have a team lunch at twelve-thirty. And then we'd train after that either back out on the field or lifting weights inside. I didn't get home until three or four most days.

It was in my third game playing for Stevenage that I felt that telltale pinch. When you tear your hamstring it's not a little pinch. It's an unmistakably strong pinch that leaves you with a dull, aching pain that sometimes hurts when you walk. There's no way to play, or even train properly, when you've got a torn hamstring. To get better you have to rest for longer than you think you have to rest. If they say one week, it's probably two. If they say one month, it's probably two. But then after you've rested, you can start riding the bike, jogging, running, and strengthening, but you have to be really careful, because hamstrings tear pretty easily—at least mine do.

I had no way of knowing, when I felt that pinch this time, that I'd be out for three months. Contrary to what I'd hoped, my life as a professional soccer player was winding down way faster than I'd expected or could have imagined. And it just happened to coincide with reaching the breaking point with my big secret. Maybe it was all that free time to think about where I was in my life and how much I hated living a lie, but without a clear focus on soccer to help me maintain my life in self-imposed exile, I was about to step across a line that I'd long ago drawn in concrete.

CHAPTER 10

WILL THEY STILL LOVE ME?

The breaking point came in early October 2012. And I knew I'd reached the breaking point because after a lifetime of keeping my sexual orientation secret I told a total stranger, a straight girl, that I was gay. My spontaneous coming out happened one evening at a bar in London's Soho neighborhood. It was the kind of place where twenty- and thirty-something professionals go after work for a drink. I'd gone right from training to meet a couple of my buddies, who brought four of their other friends, including a couple of gay guys and a stylish East London girl I'll call "Jessica." It was a quiet weekday evening and there was a mixed straight and gay crowd of maybe thirty or forty people.

We all sat at a table together and chatted. I had a beer, and since it was a work night we didn't stay long. Once we were all out on the sidewalk saying goodbye, Jessica's friends went to a cash machine while she waited with me in front of the bar, and out of the blue she said, "One of my friends fancies you. Are you straight or gay?" Without really thinking about it I said, "I'm gay." After all those years of hiding and pretending and lying I'd said, "I'm gay," to someone I'd just met. And maybe that's why I did it. Telling a complete stranger was a low-stakes dress rehearsal for what I knew was coming.

After spending so many years hiding and being afraid of what people would think if they knew I was gay, I was surprised by how easily I'd said: "I'm gay." It felt good, but it also felt weird hearing myself say it, because I'd never said it out loud before. Then Jessica asked me if I noticed all the guys at the bar who were hitting on me and I answered honestly that I didn't have a clue. To this day I never notice when someone is interested in me—a remnant, I think, from how well I'd trained myself never to be attracted to men in general. I just never allowed myself to go there.

It turned out that Jessica and I were going in the same direction and she asked if I wanted to grab a drink on the way home. If I'd been my sister Alicia I would have said, "No, thanks," because I really didn't want to go for a drink. Alicia's great at saying exactly what she thinks and feels, and she wouldn't waste energy or time with someone she doesn't want to. But I've spent my life trying to be nice, and it was almost impossible for me to say no to anything. I've come to understand that trying to please people has been my way to compensate— overcompensate is more like it—for the fact that I'm gay, which I'd perceived as such a huge negative that it needed to be compensated for. So even though I really wanted to go home, I said yes, and Jessica and I caught a bus heading for the neighborhood in East London where she lived.

Just as we were getting off the bus, Jessica's phone rang and after a brief back-and-forth she handed it to me and said, "Rob wants to talk to you." Rob was one of her friends I'd met earlier that evening, who was gay, and he said, "I just wanted you to know that Jessica is trying to hook up with you." I was stunned because I didn't have a clue. Also, it was really weird that he called tell to me. And I was shocked that Jessica wanted to hook up with me, because she knew I was gay. I've learned since that girls who are attracted to me don't seem to care whether I'm gay or not.

There was no way I was going to hook up with Jessica. Still, I didn't know how to extract myself gracefully, so after I handed the phone back to her we went to a cute little bar to hang out. I didn't tell Jessica what her friend had told me and she didn't ask, which also surprised me. We had one drink and talked about East London real estate and Jessica's work as an actress, and after about forty-five minutes it felt like enough time to say that I needed to call it a night. Once we got outside, Jessica asked me to walk her back to her place, which I knew I wasn't going to do because I didn't want to give her the impression that I was going to spend the night with her. So I walked her part-way, spotted a cab, hailed it, gave Jessica a polite hug good night, and headed home.

One of the things I discovered over the course of the evening was that Jessica's brother was a Leeds fan, so the next morning I sent her a text message saying that I liked to keep my life private and that I hoped she wouldn't say anything to her brother. I was tired of hiding, but I didn't want news of the fact that I was gay to spread from one Leeds fan to the next, and before you knew it the British tabloids would be calling my mother in California. Jessica texted me back, "Don't worry, I understand."

Despite how awkwardly the evening ended, the experience of coming out to Jessica gave me a taste of freedom and made me realize I wasn't as terrified of people knowing I was gay as I'd thought I was—which isn't to say I wasn't still very, very afraid.

Up until this point I'd planned to wait until I went home in December or January to tell my family in person, but tasting freedom made me even more eager to get out from under my huge secret. And it wasn't like I hadn't already been obsessing about it for weeks and months. I'd think about it when I woke up in the morning, while I was in the shower, while I was shaving, while I was making my breakfast, while I was on the Tube—constantly. *Am I really going to tell the truth? How am I going to do it? What will it mean for my life, for soccer? Where am I going to live? Who will I tell first? How will I tell them? What will they think?* So many questions.

With all that stuff swimming around in my head I wound up feeling trapped in my body, like I was going to suffocate if I didn't find a way out. I recognize now that a lot of my fears about coming out to my family were unfounded, especially with my siblings, but by the time I started making plans to tell my family the truth I was so stressed, anxious, and fearful that I wasn't thinking rationally. I was simply terrified, because nothing in life scared me more than the possibility of my family distancing themselves from me if they ever knew the truth. That fear drove me to do everything I could to hide, but it was long past time to make my escape from the prison I'd built for myself. It wasn't worth the price I had to pay just so I could keep playing soccer. I decided in the end that no matter how my family reacted, my life would *have* to be better on the other side.

There was one other thing that was pushing me to tell my family the truth. I needed to tell them I was gay before someone else did. I wanted to believe that Jessica would keep my secret, but I didn't think it was paranoid to imagine the story of me being gay finding its way into the media. Given that my mother and father and brother and sisters were the most important people in the world to me, for them to find out through another source would have killed me and killed them, because they could have easily thought I didn't care enough to tell them myself. Also, I wanted them to hear directly from me what an emotional thing this was for me and to tell them what I'd been through since I'd first gone into hiding. If I could explain it all to them, I knew—or at least I hoped—they'd understand.

While I was in London struggling in secret to figure out how I was going to tell my family I was gay, I was vaguely keeping tabs on the big marriage equality battle going on back at home. Just a few months before, President Obama had announced his support for same-sex marriage—something no sitting president had ever done before. Going into the election no one knew whether taking such a bold position on a hot-button social issue would help or hurt his chances of being reelected.

I read about all of this on Twitter, but it was more background noise than anything. I was so caught up in my own struggle over coming out that it didn't feel like the marriage equality fight had a lot to do with me; the thought of getting married to a man never even crossed my mind. I hadn't even been on a date with a guy! And just because the President of the United States supported marriage equality didn't meant that I'd be accepted—let alone embraced—for being gay, especially by my family.

Before I reached out to Alicia—I'd decided to tell my sister first—I thought through all the possible scenarios and ramifications. (In truth I obsessed about it more than thought about it in an organized way.) Would they feel like they didn't know me anymore? Would they wonder what this meant about my life? Would they hold it against me that I'd lied to them all this time, that I'd tried to deceive them into believing I was straight when I was really gay? Would they ever trust me again? Would they treat me differently? Would they understand? Would they reject me? Would they still love me?

Deep down I think I knew that my sisters and brother would be okay with it. They never gave me any reason to believe they wouldn't accept me. I never heard them say anything hateful about gay people. But, then, I never heard them say anything positive on the subject, either, although I'm not sure that would have made much of a difference.

With my mom, I knew she would still love me. My mom lives for her kids. But I was worried that she might not understand and would reject me initially, that she wouldn't be supportive, would distance herself and treat me differently. If she said, "I need to think about it," I would have felt devastated, because expressing any doubt about her love for me would have made me think our relationship had changed forever.

I was worried by the stories I'd heard about others in similar circumstances, like Tyler Clementi, the college student who wound up killing himself in the fall of 2010 after coming out to his parents and being spied on by his roommate when he was kissing another guy. Tyler's parents were religious and he'd told friends he felt like his mother rejected him. (It turns out that what his mom actually said was that she "needed time.")

I also remember overhearing someone tell one of my friends about how difficult it was for his mother when he came out to her. And another time I was watching a show on MTV where a gay teen said, "My mom didn't accept me at first, but then she got over it." Some people might hear that story and feel hopeful, that a mother came to accept her gay child, but all I could focus on was the initial rejection.

One thing that didn't occur to me was to do any research to see if I could get advice on how to come out to my family. I had so successfully isolated myself and screened out the gay world (except for the bad things I heard people say) that I had no idea there were gay organizations that provide all kinds of advice for people who want to come out to their parents. There's even an organization for gay Catholics. I was totally clueless, but I didn't let that stop me.

Looking back to that time, it's hard for me to remember just how scared I was. But then I remind myself of how much I had to get beyond in order to take the next step and call my sister Alicia. It was an accumulation from my whole life of all the things I'd heard in the past that made me hate myself—that left me thinking I was a fundamentally flawed, bad person. If I felt that way about myself, why wouldn't my family think the same things about me and reject me? So telling the truth meant pushing past all that fear, convincing myself that I was a good person, that God loved me as I was, and then finding the courage to at least take the first step and tell Alicia.

There was something else going through my head at that time. My decision to come out to my family was not about them. I wasn't doing this for them; this whole thing was about me. It was about me coming to terms with myself. It was about me realizing that I wasn't a bad person, that I was supposed to do good on this earth. So in the end it didn't matter what anyone else said or thought. At least that's what I told myself. Yes, I was afraid, but I needed to get this done and I needed to do it for myself.

There was never a question in my mind that Alicia would be first. She has a strong character and we love each other very much. She's the kind of person I felt comfortable talking to about everything, except the fact that I was gay. She's a very emotional person and she's acutely aware of what other people are feeling, which I'm sure is something that serves her well in her work as a nurse.

Sometimes I think Alicia is psychic, because she can sense when things aren't right. Or she'll talk about being with a patient when he's died and she can feel the energy leave the room. She's also always been in tune with everything that's going on in my life. But that didn't mean I felt one hundred percent certain about how she'd respond when I told her. What Alicia had said to me the previous Christmas about not believing in gay marriage and how she didn't know whether being gay was something you were born with or learned worried me and made me wonder. What if she told me that she still loved me but couldn't accept that I was gay? I didn't know if I could handle it if that was how she reacted.

In early November I emailed Alicia and wrote, "Hey, let's make a date to go on Skype," but I didn't let on that there was anything big I wanted to tell her. A couple of days before the call I wrote a letter, which I planned to email to Alicia once we were on Skype so she could read it on her own and then we'd talk about it. I knew that I could never say all the things I wanted to say face-to-face, even via Skype. It was a lot easier for me to write down everything than to get intensely emotional on the call, so that's how I came up with this two-step coming-out plan. In the letter I said that I'd known for a long time I was gay, that I'd been struggling, that I'd wanted to tell her earlier but I just couldn't. And I said, "This isn't something I chose, but it's something that I am. It's how I was created. It doesn't change anything." The tone of the note was almost apologetic because I felt so bad about not talking to Alicia sooner.

I was nervous writing the letter, but not nearly as nervous and scared and super-jittery as I was when I sat on my bed after practice and opened my computer to make the call. It was about three in the afternoon in London, so about seven a.m. in California where Alicia was. I'd been obsessing about the call the whole week and was lucky I didn't get run over crossing the street on my way home because I was so on edge and distracted.

My hands were sweating as I brought Skype up on my laptop screen and clicked on Alicia's number. I kept telling myself that my sister would still love me, but I worried that she'd be upset because I'd lied to her for so long. All that lying, and not just with Alicia, left me feeling totally ashamed.

Once Alicia and I were connected and said our hellos, I said, "I'm going to send you an email that you can't show anyone, that's really private. I want you to read it when we're off Skype and then call me right back." Alicia cautioned me about emailing to her AOL account. "I think Dad can look at my AOL account," she said. I didn't know how much of a risk that was, but I was so paranoid of anyone finding out without me telling them first that I told Alicia to create a Gmail account that no one else had access to, which she did, and then I sent the letter and we signed off.

As soon as I sent the email I remember thinking, *Oh, shit!* I knew deep down that Alicia would always love me, but as well as I knew her I couldn't know what she was thinking and couldn't know what she'd say. I hadn't told anyone in my family. Gosh, I hadn't told anyone in the world except for Jessica, who was basically a stranger, and I didn't care what she thought. What Alicia thought meant everything to me—if she questioned our relationship or had anything negative to say, I didn't think I could take it.

Maybe thirty seconds later Alicia called me back. I didn't think she'd had enough time to read the whole email, but when she came back on Skype I could see she had tears in her eyes. Here's what Alicia said she remembers feeling when she first read the email:

> I had a sense of relief and shame. The relief was, finally, he said it. I thought, *The truth will set you free. Thank goodness!* I was thinking maybe Robbie had been sexually abused because of the way he was hiding things. So it was also a relief that he's just gay! And I felt shame that he couldn't confide in me when he was younger, and he had to go through all that pain alone and that I couldn't protect him when my dad was yelling at him. I just wish I'd been able to hold his hand when he was little and somehow let him know he was good and it was okay. I also felt bad that in the past I'd said to Robbie that I didn't believe in gay marriage and didn't know if it was something you were born with or learned.

Knowing now how Alicia felt after reading my letter, I think she was being too hard on herself. She was a wonderful sister to me growing up and as far as marriage equality and how someone winds up gay, all of us in our family have come a long way in our thinking about all of this stuff, including me.

The first things Alicia said to me after reading the letter were, "I love you so much, Robbie. I don't care that you're gay. I'm sorry that you've had to go through all of this by yourself."

She said she was happy for me that I didn't have to struggle with this alone anymore. Alicia also asked, "What do you need from me? What do you want to do?"

I told Alicia that I needed to tell Mom, and she offered to do it for me. For a moment I thought it would be easier that way, but I knew I needed to tell Mom myself. I said, "I was thinking I'd come home in January and talk to Mom in person." Alicia was emphatic that I needed to tell her sooner, that Mom was worried about me. I told her that I'd have to think about it.

Not so surprisingly, I wasn't the only one in my family keeping secrets. Alicia didn't tell me that even before I told her I was gay, she and Mom had talked about it. She'd been having dreams about me and remembers feeling a sense of darkness around me, that something was troubling me. She told me later that in the dream I was climbing this mountain and I was wearing a big hat. We talked about what it meant, that maybe it was about me struggling, and that the big hat represented me being different.

So Alicia had mentioned to Mom that she was worried, and Mom agreed that there was "something holding Robbie back." Alicia suggested that perhaps I was gay, and they wound up having a conversation in which they sorted through all the clues and all the things that did and didn't add up, like the fact that I'd dated girls in the past. They also discussed how they should react if it turned out that what they suspected was true. That explains why Alicia wanted me to tell Mom right away, but I didn't know they'd already been talking about it. I just knew that I needed some breathing room to overcome my fears for a second time so I could tell Mom. I'd need even more courage to tell Mom than I had with Alicia, because what my mom thought and felt about me mattered more than anyone's opinion in the world. So Alicia got stuck having to fend off our mother's questions in the weeks that followed, even though she'd already learned the truth. Alicia hates lying, so I know this was painful for her and I'm sorry for having put her through that.

Alicia and I talked for probably an hour and it took most of that hour for me to calm down. It felt like I'd just climbed off a roller coaster, the adrenaline still working its way through my system. Alicia asked lots of questions: How long did I know I was gay? Was I dating anyone? Had I had a relationship in the past? It was a really easy and free-flowing conversation, which is how it's always been with her.

At the end of the call Alicia said, "Love you, Robber." I told Alicia I loved her and signed off. That night she sent me a supportive text and then we Skyped every day for a week (and every other day in the weeks after) and talked about the things we always did, but we also speculated about how various family members would react. For the most part she thought everyone would be okay with the news that I was gay, but Alicia was concerned about our mom, our dad, and our grandparents. I was most worried about my mother. Catholicism plays such a big role in our mom's life that Alicia said she just didn't know how Mom would react. That was a big question mark for both of us.

It took me weeks to get up the courage to tell my mother, but I couldn't wait forever because it wasn't fair to Alicia. I knew when I first told Alicia that once I'd told one member of my family the truth, I'd be forced to tell everyone else in my family, too.

So I took a deep breath after getting off yet one more call in which Alicia begged me to tell our mother and emailed my mom to set up a Skype date. My plan was to do the same thing as I had with Alicia: write the letter, Skype, email the letter and have Mom read it, and then Skype again.

In the letter, which I wrote in my bedroom at home after training one afternoon, I said a lot of the same things to my mother that I had written in my letter to Alicia, so it should have been easier; but given that it was my mom, it was even more challenging and nerve-wracking the second time around. Here's what I wrote:

Mom,

This is the hardest thing I have ever had to write or go through in my life.

Sometimes I think, *Why would God put me through this?*, but I have come to realize that He has a purpose for me. He has a plan for everyone obviously, and although my path will not be easy I choose to be honest.

As you might have suspected I am gay. The only reason I say you might have suspected is because you are my mom. I honestly believe moms can feel these kinds of things and we are very, very close.

I have been this way forever. I would not choose this life for myself or anyone close to me, but I have come to accept it and I am proud of the person I have become.

I have tried my whole life not to be gay, because of the way I was raised and because of my beliefs. Constantly struggling with myself has not been healthy and this has made me closed off emotionally to a lot of people.

I have dated girls, hooked up with girls, prayed, read books, all in the failing effort to try to change myself. I have come to the conclusion that this is not what He wants, nor is it what I want. After twenty-five years I have accepted myself and I have realized I was created this way for a reason.

As you know God created us all with our different talents and skills. He created us to be different, and because of this I can't believe the life He chose for me is a life of sin.

I know I am a good person. I care for people, love my family and friends.

I am gay and I have to break barriers and be the same person that I have always been.

I am sorry I had to write this to you but it would be too hard for me to tell you in person mainly because I know that this is a disappointment for you.

I want you to know I will always be the same person. My beliefs have not changed. I still believe in the same life principles.

My whole life I have felt alone because of this and I believe I am ready to be open with people.

I want you to know you can tell as many people as you want and if you don't want to tell anyone, as well, I 100% understand that.

I am sure Grandpa and Grammers won't understand but in time I think people will realize I am still the same good person.

Again, I know this will be hard for you to come to terms with, but I will always love you no matter what.

Lets talk this over, but I had to put it into words first so you could understand how I am feeling.

Love your Son,
Robbie

I read that letter now and can feel how much I was still struggling to come to terms with who I was, and I can see how a lot of what I wrote in that letter was for me, not my mom. As much as I needed to tell my mother that I was a good person and that this was how God created me, I needed to tell myself, too. I can also see what a long way I'd come from the days when I prayed for God to make me straight.

When I emailed my mother to tell her I wanted to Skype, I wrote, "Hey mom, I need to talk to you about something." I don't know if she knew anything was up. In the past I would have said the same thing and the "something" could have been anything from soccer stuff to "I need help with my taxes." I Skyped with my mom a lot, so maybe she could feel that this was different. I've always felt really connected to my mom and we've had what's felt like a special relationship, but I also struggled in my relationship with her because I couldn't share so much of what was going on inside me and was afraid she wouldn't like this side of me because of her religious beliefs.

For my mom, church comes first. She goes to mass every single day. She speaks at mass. She reads the Bible. She says the rosary every night. I could only imagine it would be a challenge for her to have a son whose very identity was disapproved of by her Church. I know that's not the case with everyone. There are a lot of Catholics who don't agree with the Church about a lot of things, but my mom is very committed to the principles of the Catholic Church and I was afraid that because of her beliefs she would wonder whether I'd be going to hell because I was gay.

When I sat down to Skype with my mom I was even more anxious and scared than I had been with my sister. My heart was pounding hard in my chest like it was trying to escape. I could feel the sweat dripping off my scalp and down my back. But despite my state of mind I was determined to be strong during the call. What I wanted to project was *This is who I am and this is how God made me*, which is a belief that took me years to embrace. I didn't want my mother to think this was something I'd just decided on a whim. And I didn't want her to think I thought that being gay was a bad thing, or that I was upset about being gay, despite how much I'd struggled in the past.

I called my mom on Skype and as soon as she was on I said, "Mom, I need to talk to you about something." Right away I could see a look of concern on her face. She didn't look worried, just focused in the way that she always was when I asked her for help. I explained to her that I'd written a letter and was going to email it. I said, "Can you read it and call me right back?" She said okay and we signed off.

I talked to my mom later about what it was like for her reading my letter, and here's what she remembers:

I didn't read the letter once. I read it a couple of times. It contained such a potpourri of feelings, and experiencing those feelings felt almost like an avalanche. It was an answer. It was an explanation. It was a relief. Finally this is here. It was almost exciting because this was a new beginning. But I was also filled with anxiety and fear. What does this mean? Does this mean he's not going to be a part of my life? Or does he mean that this is who I am and let's go forward? And I was left wondering, *How can I not have been there for him? How did I fail in letting Robbie know that I loved him no matter what?*

While I sat waiting for my mom to call back, I was so anxious and scared that I just stared at the computer waiting for it to ring with my Mom's call. After two minutes it rang. When Mom came up on my computer screen she looked so calm and peaceful that I let go of the breath I hadn't realized I'd been holding. She said, "Robbie, I love you so much. It doesn't matter to me." As soon as I heard those words I started crying—crying with relief from having told her, and crying with appreciation for her love and support. I said, "Mom, I didn't expect to be so emotional." I told her I wasn't expecting such support from her right off the bat. And then Mom was crying, too. She said, "I hate that you had to struggle for so long about this on your own."

My mother also told me something that she'd said many times in the past, that I was a gift from God and that God made me perfect. Whenever she'd said that before, I always wondered, *What would she say if she knew how* not *perfect I was?* But now she knew the whole truth about me and she was still saying it. Honestly, I was shocked and confused, because it was so *not* what I had expected to hear.

We must have Skyped for an hour after that. We talked about everything from who I wanted to tell to what I was going to do about soccer. I told Mom that at the end of the year I was going to walk away. I wasn't going to tell anyone why I was retiring from soccer. I said, "I'm going to be Robbie Rogers who is no longer a soccer player and I'm going to apply to fashion design school." I explained that I didn't want to be the poster boy for gay athletes, that I just wanted to have my life for the first time in my life.

Mom also asked me if I wanted her to tell anyone. I told her that I was planning to tell my brother and other two sisters and she asked if it would be okay with me if she talked to my brother, Tim, before I did. My mother thought it would be easier for Tim if she told him in person than for me to tell him via Skype. Mom is very protective of us and our relationships with each other and I know she felt better doing it that way.

So that left my two other sisters, my father, and my grandparents. Mom asked me how I wanted to tell her parents, Grandpa and Grammers, and I said I wanted to tell them in person when I came home—I was extremely concerned about disappointing them, especially given that they're very traditional and conservative midwestern Catholics. We agreed that I'd tell Dad later because I was afraid he might not keep my confidence while I figured out what to do about soccer. I also said that I'd let Dad tell his parents himself. I love my father's parents, but they live in Ann Arbor, Michigan, so I only saw them about once a year when I was growing up. And for that reason I was more comfortable letting him talk to them, and I figured I'd follow up by writing to them after.

My mom had remarried, and I told her that it was up to her if she wanted to tell her husband, Jeff. I'd heard homophobic things from Jeff in the past, so I wasn't eager to have that conversation. Two years prior I'd overheard a conversation in which Jeff and my mother were talking about two men getting married, and Jeff said, "If they want to get married I don't want to go to a gay wedding." But that was really nothing compared to the big blowup we'd had when I was fourteen or fifteen. Jeff asked me if I had a girlfriend and when I said that I didn't he said, "What, are you gay?" I got really mad and defensive because by then I knew I was gay and was terrified that he'd blow my cover. I challenged him and said in a really angry voice, "Why would you ask me that? Why would you even bring it up?" In the end I wound up apologizing to him for losing my temper and he said it was "very manly" of me to apologize, and he apologized in turn. So I didn't think he'd be surprised that I was gay, but I didn't feel comfortable talking about it with him.

My mother also asked if I'd had any relationships in the past (I hadn't), and she asked how I felt about same-sex marriage and if I ever wanted to get married and have a kid. I said, "Mom, I have no idea. I'm just trying to figure out things one day at a time." And it wasn't like I could have gotten legally married in California at that time even if I'd had someone special in my life and wanted to. It would be another seven months before the U.S. Supreme Court overturned Prop 8 and cleared the way for same-sex marriages in my home state. (I couldn't have gotten legally married to a man in the UK, either, in November 2012, but in July 2013 Britain legalized same-sex marriage.)

At the end of the hour I think we were both wrung out. Before we ended the call Mom said, "If you need to talk to me about anything, just give me a call. I love you and you need to know that I'm supporting you. I'm just happy that you felt you could tell us now."

I said, "Thank you. I love you."

It's hard to describe the feeling I had when I got off the phone—a powerful mix of euphoria, relief, and exhaustion—but mostly I was thrilled. I remember thinking, *Wow! I just did that!* I was so happy to know that I was still my mom's son and that being gay didn't change our relationship at all. It felt like the best day of my life!

For the next few weeks Mom and I Skyped every day and she texted me all the time. In subsequent days we talked about the usual things, like my life in London, my friends, my sister's pregnancy. Just normal chat, but even though most of the things we talked about were the things we had talked about before I came out, it was qualitatively different for me. I could be myself, relaxed and unguarded. I didn't have to monitor everything I said to make sure I didn't say anything that would give me away. I didn't have to be on high alert that my mom would ask me something I couldn't answer or would have to lie about. I could be honest. While I wouldn't go out of my way to say that I'd gone out to a gay bar, one time when Mom asked me what I'd done the night before, I told her, "Yeah, I went out to this gay bar and met some people . . ." I described the people I had seen and how different gay people were from each other.

I talked about how there's this stereotyped view that all gay people are the same or similar, but just like at straight clubs, you see every type of person.

Through the whole conversation Mom was right there with me. She wasn't judgmental and she'd be the first person to say that God created us all to be different. Sometimes Mom would laugh about the funny stories I told her about my experiences going out. Just as it was all new to me, it was all so new for her, too. It was great to be able to share these things with my mom as I explored them. For a change I didn't feel so alone, and that felt really good.

The one time I went on high alert was when Mom told me she'd talked with her priest. I thought, *Uh-oh, I wonder what he had to say.* But then she told me what he said: "Theresa, this isn't about you and your son and your relationship with God. This is about your son and *his* relationship with God. From what I know about your son, he's a lovely boy who a lot of people enjoy being around. Stop worrying about him and just love him." I agreed with the priest that my relationship with God was nobody's business but my own. I could tell from the way my mother told me about her conversation with the priest that she was relieved, but I still think she worries about whether I'll go to heaven.

Although I shared a lot with my mother in the weeks that followed, I didn't share everything. Between the time I came out to my sister and when I talked to my mother, I'd met a man I liked. He's a private person (although totally open about being gay), so I'll call him "Scott." I didn't talk to my mom about meeting Scott or going on dates with him. I didn't know how serious it was, so it didn't seem appropriate or necessary to say anything. I'd remembered my brother and sisters bringing home people they weren't serious about and thinking, *Why bother?* For me to bring someone home to meet my mom and my dad and my brother and sisters it would have to be a pretty serious relationship.

But really, I just wasn't ready to deal with that amount of personal detail. It was one thing to say I was gay, but a whole other thing to talk about having a boyfriend. I was still so uncomfortable myself going on my first few dates with Scott, and I had no idea where the relationship was going. I couldn't imagine having to talk about that on top of everything else I'd just talked about. I was already answering a lot of questions and this seemed like too much. If it got serious, then I'd have to say something. After finally coming out, I didn't want to fall back into hiding the truth about my life, but I came to realize that coming out didn't mean I forfeited a zone of privacy. It would take me a while to figure out how far out that zone extended, but at least for now I decided that I didn't need to talk with my family about Scott.

One thing my mom wanted to talk about that I definitely did *not* want to talk about was anything to do with my sex life, and I don't think that's much different from any mother and son whether or not he's gay. But just because it wasn't something I didn't want to talk about didn't mean it was something my mother would just let go, not given her close-up experience helping friends and clients who had AIDS and the fact that she's a nurse and a lawyer. Mom could tell I was uncomfortable with that conversation, so when it became clear I wasn't going to engage her, she simply said, "I may not be the person that you talk to about this, but there is no option that you remain ignorant. So choose in any way that you want to become edu-cated, but become educated." I could hardly argue with my mother, because that's the kind of advice I would give to any young person who is thinking about becoming sexually active.

I learned an important lesson from my experience of coming out to my mother. And it was something that I came to discover was also true about a lot of my fellow soccer players when I later went public about being gay. Even though my mom had said things in the past that led me to believe she was homopho-bic, deep down she really wasn't someone who hated gay people. In fact, if I'd been paying more attention I would have realized that some of my mother's friends and clients were gay (as I'm sure that some of my teammates had friends and family who were gay). But at the time I just couldn't see it, because I'd made assumptions about my mother and her views because of my own stereotypes about people who are traditionally reli-gious. I should have known better. Sorry, Mom.

A short time after I told my mother, I told my youngest sister, Katie, and I did it in the same way I told my mom and Alicia. You might think—and I might have thought—that after telling Alicia and Mom that I was gay and having it go so well, I wouldn't be afraid anymore of telling anyone. I only wish that were true! I've discovered that this kind of fear does not go away overnight, especially when you've been scared for as long as I'd been scared. So I was still nervous telling Katie, although not as nervous as the first two times. Katie is brilliant. She's this blond, beautiful girl and she writes the darkest stories. She's really creative and thinks differently from a lot of people I know. I couldn't imagine that she would have a problem with me being gay.

It turns out that Katie was at Starbucks when we Skyped, so it wasn't ideal for a long conversation, especially since it wasn't a good connection. Again I used the same routine but I wrote a much shorter note to Katie than I had to Alicia and Mom. In it I said, "Katie, I love you and I know you're not going to care that I'm gay. You're just such a lovely and amazing person and the only reason I didn't tell you first was I knew you'd be okay with it." Katie called me back on Skype and she was crying. She said, "I'm just so happy." I asked her why and she said, "I'm so happy that you're happy now, that you've come to this place in your life." And after that we just talked about normal stuff, the routine fabric of our daily lives. That was the easiest.

Around the same time I told Katie, my mom told my brother and he sent me an email. In it he said, "Robbie, I just want you to know I love you and look up to you and this doesn't change anything. I have so much respect for you as a person." I wrote back and simply said, "Thank you *so* much for sending this to me." It wasn't a big deal for Tim, which itself was a really big deal to me. And it was just about the same with my sister Nicole. What I worried most about with Coco was that she'd feel bad that I told her last of my siblings, but she didn't seem to mind. She was the only one of my siblings to tell me, after I told her, that she'd thought I might be gay because, as she said, "You're a well-dressed, good-looking guy, and you never had a relationship." As clueless as I still was about being gay, I knew enough to know that not all gay people dress well, and gay people come in all shapes and sizes and look no different from anyone else. In the moment I was tempted to correct my sister, but I decided to save that discussion for another time.

I waited two months from when I told my mother until I talked to my father. He was the last person of my immediate family I told, and he was unhappy about that. I knew he would be, which was why I was especially nervous telling him. But I didn't think he'd have a problem with me being gay. Even though I'd heard some homophobic things from him in the past, he'd changed a lot since I was younger. If you asked him what his religious beliefs are now, he'd tell you that there are many pathways to heaven. When he was still with my mom he was devoutly Catholic.

I sent my dad an email and then I talked with him by phone. I didn't give him a heads-up that I wanted to discuss something important. I just wrote an email and said that this was what I'd been struggling with and that one of the reasons it was hard for me to tell him was because it was man-to-man. I explained that most boys want to grow up to be like their dads. I wrote, "It was a little harder for me to say this to you, because in a fundamental way I'm not like you."

In my email I also I apologized for telling my father last and I explained why. I said, "From my past experiences of sharing things with you that I had thought were in confidence but turned out not to be, I couldn't trust that you could keep yourself from telling anyone." I hadn't yet decided how long I was going to wait before making a public statement—or whether I'd even make a public statement—but however long that was, I knew that once my father knew, it would be difficult for him to keep it to himself. I was pretty sure he'd tell his sister and his parents and they'd share it with others. That sort of thing had happened before when I told my father relatively inconsequential things about soccer and he shared them with his family before I was ready for them to know. Then I'd lose control of it and I'd hate that and wind up being really mad at him. Whether that was a realistic concern this time around or not, that's what I was afraid of at the time, and I decided to be honest with my father about it even though I knew it would hurt his feelings.

Other than being upset with me for telling everyone before telling him, my dad was great. During our phone call he said, "I hate that you had to struggle for so long about this on your own" and that it pained him to know I'd been so alone. Since then we've been in regular communication, just as we were before I told him, so nothing's really changed except that I was relieved I could be myself with him and talk about everything, just like I could be myself with my mother and brother and sisters.

In some ways it all felt too easy, but that's not the kind of thing you can complain about. So I just thanked God for my family and felt like a very lucky man, especially knowing that not every gay person is accepted by his or her family in the way that I've been embraced by mine.

After I told Alicia I was gay I started telling my friends, too, from across the spectrum of my life. I've really been blessed because I've lived in a lot of places and along the way made some really good friends, mostly men and mostly straight. I was nervous with everyone. Even when things went well, which they did with every one of the twenty or so friends I told before the end of 2012, it made me nervous to have "the conversation," and sometimes I'd make a date to meet up with a friend and then I'd wind up being too afraid and I'd have to try again the next time.

Two friends, Warren and Andy, stand out, mostly because I told them early on, so the experience was still new to me. I'd known Warren for two years, and Andy and I lived next door to each other when we played for the Columbus Crew. Andy and I met when I was nineteen and he was twenty-three, and we played soccer together for a few years. Andy is straight and Warren is gay. I know, how could I be nervous telling a gay friend I was gay? But I was. It wasn't so much that I was afraid Warren would judge me because I was gay, but I was afraid he'd be upset with me for lying to him. And even if he was upset, I didn't think he'd be *that* upset, but it was just so hard to get those words out of my mouth: I'm gay.

Andy was the first friend I told. I texted him and told him I was going to email him a letter and then we talked on Skype. In my letter I talked about my faith, my family, and about soccer, about struggling my whole life and accepting that this is who I am. When he called, he was incredibly supportive and said, "I'm so proud of you. When we first met, you were this successful and spoiled soccer player who always got what he wanted. And over time I've seen you struggle through your career with different challenges. I'm so happy that you've grown up enough and matured enough to recognize that this isn't a big deal and now you're ready to move on. And whatever it takes, you're willing to be honest."

Andy told me that he always thought I might be gay but it

wasn't something he was going to ask me. He said, "You could get whatever girl you wanted, but you weren't interested in going out or doing any of that stuff, so it seemed pretty clear to me. Now you're willing to break down barriers and be who you are. When people realize who you are and that you're the same good person you've always been, a lot of kids are going to be able to connect with your experience." I remember being in a panic when Andy said that, because I couldn't yet wrap my mind around the idea of coming out publicly and absorbing the reactions of people who didn't know me.

It was great being able to talk to Andy, because he was one of my best friends and he lived in London. Whenever we saw each other after that he always had questions for me: Are you dating anyone? Who have you told? Who are you going to tell? Are you going to release a statement? Do you think you'll go back to soccer after you've come out? So he was someone I always felt comfortable talking to, and I was going to need his advice and support as I figured out what to do about my career in soccer.

I told Warren second. He lives in Los Angeles and he and his husband, James, are now among my closest friends. They have a place just down the street from me in West Hollywood. Back in November 2012, they were visiting their families in the UK (we had Thanksgiving together) and I couldn't believe how nervous I was to begin the conversation. But I finally managed to do it while we were walking through London's Hyde Park on a rare sunny day. I told Warren that I had something to tell him. Like Alicia, he's a pretty tuned-in person, and he said later that as soon as I said I had something to tell him he knew what I was going to say.

I said, "Warren, we've been good friends and I don't know

why it's so hard for me to say this because you're gay, but I'm gay." His reaction was totally understated. He gave me a hug and told me that he had the feeling I was, and that James thought I was, and then he basically said, "So, what's next?" I told him I was probably going to step away from soccer, which he understood because he used to play and knows how homophobic soccer can be. And that was pretty much it. I have to admit that I was surprised by Warren's reaction. I wasn't expecting him to be dramatic, like, *Are you okay?* But I also didn't expect him to be so low-key. In my head it was such a big thing, but he was so relaxed about it, which made me think that maybe one day I might come to think that it wasn't such a big thing after all. (I'm not there yet.)

After I talked with my mother and sister, they both said I looked twenty pounds lighter. And I'm sure I looked even less burdened after my brother, two other sisters, father, and many of my friends knew, too. But as relieved as I was for all of them to now know the real Robbie Rogers—and I was massively relieved!—I knew it was only the beginning of a challenging journey. Still, the worst was behind me. As I came to learn, starting the "coming-out conversation" is the hardest part, and however fearful I'd been and still am about how people will feel about me once they knew the truth, nothing will ever be as difficult as telling the most important people in the world to me that I'm gay. I only wish I'd risked confiding in them sooner.

CHAPTER 11

FIRST TIME

By November 2012 my life was changing so fast and I was experiencing so many profoundly new things that I don't know how I kept it all together and even managed to play soccer again (although not memorably) after recovering from my hamstring tear. I'd finally embraced the fact that I was gay, taken the huge step of coming out to my sister (though this was when I was still procrastinating about telling my mother), and was exploring London and a life outside of soccer through an internship with Trace Publicity.

And then I met Scott.

I don't think I was out there looking for a boyfriend, but I was definitely open to that possibility in a way I'd never been before. I had known I was gay since my early teens, and here I was at the age of twenty-five and I had yet to kiss a guy for the first time. If ever there was a poster boy for people who say you don't need to have any physical experience to know that you're gay, I'm it.

I met Scott while I was working a "press day" for Trace Publicity. It was a cocktail reception where fashion magazine editors, public relations folks, and other people from the fashion industry come in to have a look at the clothing brands you have on display. I was hanging out and talking with a group of people when one of my friends introduced me to Scott. He said, "This is Robbie. He's an intern at Trace. And he's a footballer, a professional athlete." From what I could tell, Scott couldn't have cared less. But he also might have just been confused, which happened to me all the time while I was interning, because people I met had a hard time understanding why a professional soccer player would also be an intern for a company that does fashion PR. To me it was pretty straightforward. I wanted to learn. But it didn't fit with how people thought of professional athletes and certainly not an American "footballer" living in London.

Scott and I talked for a little while about living in London and what I was doing there. My first impression of Scott was that he was an attractive, nice guy and I liked talking to him. Later in the evening, we talked again, mostly about Scott's new dog, Dougal. He'd brought him along and I'd been playing with him. And that was pretty much it. At some point I looked around and realized that Scott had left.

When I got home that night I sent Scott a friend request on Facebook and said, "Let's grab a coffee sometime." Pretty tame stuff, but in some ways that was the most radical thing I'd ever done or written in my entire life. Before then, I never would have approached a guy I knew was gay, especially someone I found attractive. But I thought, *I'm allowed to do this.*

We had just lost to Nigeria at the 2008 Olympics in Beijing. This is what dashed Olympic dreams look like.

Everything about the Columbus Crew's 2008 season exceeded everyone's expectations, including my own. We'd just won the MLS Cup in Los Angeles against the NY Red Bulls. Feeling a huge sense of accomplishment, I couldn't resist showing how I felt about the MLS Cup itself.

In a 2011 game against the LA Galaxy, battling with the legendary David Beckham.

Playing in 2011 for the U.S. National team (under coach Jürgen Klinsmann for the first time), in a game against Mexico in Tampa, Florida, I scored a goal, which led to a 1–1 draw.

After scoring a goal for Columbus Crew I celebrated with my teammate Eddie Gaven at our home field in Columbus, Ohio, in 2011.

My sister Alicia's wedding in 2012. I was just back from Leeds in the United Kingdom following surgery to repair my broken ankle. Happy for my sister and happy to be home with my family, but struggling with myself over whether to tell them the truth about my life. *From left to right:* me, Mom, Timmy, Alicia, Katie, and Coco.

Having fun with my dog Jeffrey at Google's offices in London, in March 2013, when I did a Google Hangout with reporters from the U.K.'s *Guardian* and the *New York Times*. It was my first time talking with the media about being gay and coming out. It felt good to finally talk about all that stuff.

At a home game in 2013 with the LA Galaxy. After years of hiding, I'm back to being the happy Robbie Rogers.

Proud, excited, and filled with love for my first niece. At my sister Alicia's house in July 2013 with baby Lily.

Celebrating my LA Galaxy teammate Sean Franklin's goal during the 2013 playoffs against Real Salt Lake. We won that game 1–0 in the first round of playoffs.

In October 2013, I had the honor of cochairing the annual GLSEN Respect Awards ceremony in Los Angeles, with my friend Jason Collins, the out and proud NBA player. I was so happy that my family— including my grandparents— was there to support me. (GLSEN is one of my favorite organizations because education is key to helping LGBT kids and all young people move the ball forward in the fight for a world free from discrimination.)

Fooling around with a soccer ball in the middle of a fashion photo shoot, styled by my friend Warren Baker, for *Flaunt* magazine.

Scott responded the next day and we made a date to meet at the flower market in East London, which was his suggestion. You might have thought this whole thing would have made me nervous, considering that it was going to be the first real date of my life, but until I was actually on my way to meet up with Scott I was totally calm. Well, I was probably nervous before that because I can remember exactly what I chose to wear that day, which is something I never remember.

First, I should explain that I always think about what I wear. In London, where I was around fashion people all the time, I made even more of an effort to look nice. So that Sunday afternoon, knowing that I wanted to make a positive impression, I put yet more thought into what I was going to wear. In the end I chose black jeans and a white Stephan Schneider knit top (which was similar to one I saw in the movie *A Single Man*). I wore a wax canvas jacket and pair of old, beat-up black Cole Haan boots.

I think I had good reasons to be nervous. I'd never done anything like that before in my life. I didn't know what to anticipate. And I didn't know how Scott was going to act. In general I'm not really nervous meeting or speaking with people one-on-one, but this was different. As casual as I'd made it sound to Scott, this wasn't just going for a coffee, although as far as I could tell that's what Scott thought it was. (I learned later that he didn't even know I was gay until he'd asked mutual friends, and then wasn't sure he believed them.)

So we met at the flower market and went for a coffee. We talked about his work, about my internship and fashion, and then at some point I told him I was gay, explained what I was going through, and that I was thinking about quitting soccer. I don't know exactly how it came up, but probably I just wanted to talk about it, so I brought it up. Talking about being gay was still so new to me that I found it hard to do. Scott was cool about it, but didn't say a lot and didn't have any opinion about what I should do about soccer.

Long after we finished our coffees Scott suggested that we get something to eat, so we headed out and we found a really cool pub at the top of Broadway Market, in the Hackney area. We had a roast (I had a vegetarian roast, which is vegetables cooked in the oven) and Yorkshire pudding. And after a few beers I was chill and not nervous at all. We had a great time talking and joking and laughing. We found that we had a lot in common even though he's from Scotland and quite a few years older than I am. We never talked about soccer, which was great. I don't know what makes someone connect with someone else, but it was easy to talk with Scott and it felt like there was something there between us, a spark.

I was having such a good time that we stayed at the pub after dinner and had more drinks. I was so drunk by the time we left that I somehow lost my keys and wallet without noticing until after Scott dropped me off in front of my place (we'd taken a cab) and he continued on to his place. I have no memory of how we said goodbye, but I remember climbing out onto the balcony next to my front door and crawling in through the window, which, thank God, was open. I was very lucky I didn't fall, because even though it was only one story up I still could have broken my neck or my ankle. Again.

It wasn't until our third date that we hooked up. We went for dinner at a place near my apartment and then I invited him back to my house for tea. He said yes. I knew by then where that was leading and I wanted it to lead there. I was attracted to Scott. Also, I remember thinking, *I'm allowed to do this. I'm a gay man and I should be able to date a man I like.* And so far, I liked Scott, which meant there was no reason not to ask him back to my place. Still, I was nervous because I'd never kissed a guy before, let alone had sex.

We were in my kitchen making tea and I don't remember what we were talking about, but he was teasing me and said something like, "I can tell you're new at this," which felt like a playful challenge and an invitation. So I kissed him, which he welcomed. And while we kissed I remember thinking, *Oh, this is different*, which on a purely physical level it *was*. Scott had facial hair, so he was scruffy, and he was, well, a guy. The girls I'd kissed were very feminine, and fragile and petite. Scott was bigger than I was and muscular in a way that no girl I'd ever kissed was. So it was all this stuff I wasn't used to, but it got normal pretty quick because I was kissing someone I was attracted to, someone I actually wanted to kiss.

The whole experience of kissing Scott was enjoyable, especially in comparison to when I was kissing a girl at some party. When I kissed a girl I had so many things going through my mind other than what I was in the middle of doing. I'd be thinking, *I'm not enjoying this. I'm just trying to cover for being gay. Am I doing this right? Can she tell I'm gay? What's going on in the other room? Let's get this over with.* But when I was kissing Scott, I wanted to be there. I wanted to kiss him. Kissing him was a sexually intimate thing, and I'd never experienced that before in my entire life. It makes me sad to think I'd waited so long to experience something that should have been a natural part of my adolescence, but instead it was forbidden to me because I thought it would ruin my life.

If kissing Scott was a bit awkward at first, having sex for the first time was even more awkward because I was so inexperienced. But like kissing, sex with Scott felt right and it got normal fast. It felt like, *This is supposed to be my life. I'm supposed to feel this way.* It was so clear to me that this was the normal and natural thing for me to do. And unlike when I had sex with girls, I wasn't thinking, *When are you leaving?* I wanted Scott to stay, which he did.

After all those years of feeling bad about being gay and pushing down my feelings until I felt almost nothing, you might think that the next morning, sitting across my kitchen table from Scott having breakfast, I might have felt regret or guilt or something bad. But instead I felt fine. I was happy that Scott was there and that we could make breakfast together. What I felt guilty about was thinking back to when I hooked up with girls and how I used them to prove to myself and people around me that I wasn't gay. And I felt sad—and still feel sad—that I had sex with girls in the hope that they'd somehow help make me straight. I never kissed a girl or hooked up with a girl because I wanted to. I feel sorry for how I used them and I feel sad that I ever believed it was the only option I had.

After that first time with Scott it wasn't like I automatically knew how to have a relationship. I can't imagine it was easy for Scott to deal with a twenty-five-year-old teenager. And, honestly, as much as I wanted to have a boyfriend, I was coping with so many different things at once during the weeks and months that we were in a relationship that I'm sure I wasn't always a lot of fun.

In the beginning I felt pretty clueless about how to be around Scott, whether we were sitting on the couch together or preparing dinner in the kitchen. It wasn't like I didn't know how men and women acted with each other romantically—if nothing else, I'd seen plenty of movies—but with a guy I wasn't even certain about how you showed affection. I had to learn every aspect of being in a relationship. So for the first month I got a lot wrong, but with Scott's help I figured it out, and over time learned plenty about what it means to share your life with another person, like being in constant contact with someone and actually caring about them and being interested in their day and sharing your feelings, which was the toughest for me. I wasn't very good at showing emotions and I'm still not, although I'm getting better.

However much of a novice I was at having a relationship, we very quickly fell into a routine of doing things together. We would ride our bikes everywhere and do the flea markets. We'd go shopping, go out to eat, see movies, hang out at the house and cook, go to the gym, and go to yoga together. It was nice just being able to share my life and thoughts with someone who really knew who I was. That was the best thing—not having to hide anything, at least when we were alone at my place or his.

One big challenge was how to behave in public, because I still wasn't really out. I was afraid that if anyone saw us together my cover would be blown. I know I overcompensated by keeping more distance from Scott than I needed to when we were in public, which understandably upset him. It's not like I walked on the other side of the street, but I wasn't even able to walk comfortably with him the way I normally would with a friend. Some of that was my own homophobia. When you grow up learning that being gay is something bad, you wind up feeling so ashamed that you wouldn't want to do anything that would make other people think you were gay, even if those people were total strangers and didn't mean anything to you. So you wind up overcompensating in a way that's hurtful to the person you're with. It's something I still find a struggle even though I'm now totally out.

With Scott I wasn't just being paranoid about being recognized, because one time it happened. I was at a straight bar with him one night when we ran into some Leeds fans who wanted to take my picture. I wasn't really worried that they'd think we were in a relationship because there was nothing about the way we interacted that would suggest we were a couple (I made sure of that), but it left me with this weird feeling that I'd just had my picture taken with my boyfriend by the kinds of fans I wasn't so sure would be supportive of me if they knew I was gay.

During the first couple of months I was seeing Scott, before the soccer season ended, the contrast between my life in the locker room and my relationship with Scott sometimes made my head spin. In the locker room I'd hear my teammates at Stevenage talk with each other about gay relationships: "How could a man have sex with a man?" "Why on earth would a man want to?" "How could a man fall in love with a man?" It made me wonder how they could be so ignorant—and made me wonder, as well, what they would think of me if they knew I was doing the things they found so unimaginable.

It turned out that I wouldn't have to wonder for much longer.

CHAPTER 12

THE TRUTH WILL SET YOU FREE

The nail in the coffin came in December, when I was finally back playing for Stevenage after my hamstring tear healed. One of the coaches said flat-out, "You guys are passing the ball like faggots." That made me so mad and I wanted to say in response, "Oh, really? What does a faggot pass a ball like?" Of course, I was still closeted, so I couldn't say anything, but it made me feel like these people didn't have any idea what they were saying. They didn't know anything about gay people. They didn't care how their words might cut. Even worse, it didn't even occur to them. And here's this guy who the young players look up to and he's setting the example that this is how you're supposed to inspire your players. Threaten them by calling them faggots. That's some inspiration, and it made me think, *This sport isn't for me.* And by then I'd already come out to my family, so I was like, *I'm so done with this.*

There was of course another option. I could have challenged the coach. I could have said I was gay. But that was beyond anything I could imagine. As far as I was concerned there was no way I could play as an out gay man. Not in the UK. Not anywhere. Maybe someone else would have had the strength to step out of the closet and right back onto the field and absorb whatever reaction there was from his teammates, the fans, and from the media. But I wasn't that person. I knew enough about myself to know what I could handle and what I couldn't. So I would step away from soccer and fade into a normal life. I'd go back to school and if I wanted I could work at a coffee shop or restaurant on the side. I liked the idea of just being a regular person.

The season was just about over with Stevenage. I'd been injured a lot, hardly played, my mind was elsewhere, and whatever dreams I'd had of using my time with Stevenage as a way back into the Championship League had evaporated. Because I'd played so infrequently, I had no opportunity to demonstrate what I was capable of doing. Instead, the only thing I'd managed to do during my few months with Stevenage was demonstrate how prone I was to injury. All I could focus on now was coming out and getting as far away from soccer as possible.

Unfortunately, I couldn't just walk away, because I was still under contract to Leeds United. Getting out of my contract was something my agent, Shaun Higgins, was going to have to help me with, so I sent him an email and said, "We need to have a serious talk." I was so nervous about telling Shaun I was gay that it never occurred to me that based on the tone of my email he might have thought I was going to fire him (which was what he told me later he'd feared). Even though I'd come out to two dozen people by then, when I sat down with Shaun a few days later at a coffee shop near Covent Garden, I was scared and sweaty and jittery and hyper-aware of everything going on around me. It was like I was about to be eaten alive by some creature I couldn't see.

I knew that once I could get the conversation started I'd be okay, but it was the anticipation that left me agitated and with a cramp in my stomach. You would think that, given the fact I hadn't had a single bad reaction up to now, I wouldn't have been such a mess, but I was still afraid of how Shaun might react. He could say something awful or he might not understand, and that terrified me. It was that way with everyone I'd come out to.

As soon as Shaun walked into the coffee shop I gave him a hug—I'd known him since I was fourteen, and when we were younger we'd played on the Orange County Blue Star together, so he was a friend, too. At first we talked about random things like my injuries and my family. Then I took a deep breath and told him I was gay. I explained that I'd told my parents and that I wanted him to talk with Leeds because I wanted out of my contract.

I was relieved when the first thing Shaun said was "It doesn't matter to me." Then he said he was sorry and that he wished he could have helped me when I was younger. But what he said next made me think he didn't get what I was going through. He said, "You should continue to play." At first I was angry because he didn't understand. And to be fair, he wasn't gay, so how could he know what a living hell my life had been?

So I tried explaining. I asked Shaun to imagine what it would be like going back into the locker room or going out on the field once everyone knew I was gay. What scared me most was the thought of being in the locker room and being treated differently, that my teammates would walk on eggshells and treat me like an outcast. I told him I was worried that my teammates would be afraid to shower with me or they'd walk out of the shower room when I walked in. The thought of going into an environment with my teammates where no one wanted to be with me scared the shit out of me.

I'd worked so hard to fit in, and now I could easily imagine being frozen out. If I'd been playing for a U.S. team I'm not sure I would have been as afraid, but given what soccer is like in the UK, I felt certain it would be a bad situation for me. Then I talked to Shaun about how difficult it had been for me hiding all those years. And I said that I needed time to figure out how to be myself, as a gay man, away from soccer and out of the spotlight.

Maybe I wasn't good at explaining myself or maybe my experience was just too unknowable for Shaun, but two or three more times during our conversation he told me that I should keep playing. I know it was coming from a good place, but I just wanted to tell Shaun to "shut the fuck up." Instead I said as firmly as I could, "I'm done. You need to talk to Leeds."

You might think that after all of the hard work, all the training, the highs and lows, the championships, the cheering fans, and all the strokes I got from my family and friends for being Robbie Rogers the professional soccer player, I might have felt a moment's regret when Shaun called me to tell me it was done, that I was no longer under contract to Leeds. Not a single regret, at least not then. I was just focused on enjoying my life in London, spending time with Scott and my friends, and learning about magazine publishing at my new internship in the fashion department at *Men's Health* magazine.

One thing I had to do, if I was going to go back to school to study fashion as I'd said I wanted to, was submit my application for the London College of Fashion. It turned out to be a much more challenging process than I'd expected. I already had experience with fabrics and fit because of my work with Halsey, but that wasn't nearly enough. They wanted me to prove that I was creative, too. So I had to demonstrate that I could sketch and develop mood boards. (A mood board is a collage of images and colors that you use as inspiration to create your clothing line.)

I wound up having a total of three interviews in which I presented my mood boards, and each time the interviewer (who was the same person each time) asked me to do some more work and come back again. One of my mood boards was based on the architecture of New York City, and I used conflicting patterns made up of different styles of building windows. For my other mood board I used a lot of African patterns and colors and played with different kinds of flowers, with an eye toward creating a clothing line that was structured but colorful.

The whole experience of applying to school was scary, and I was especially nervous for the interviews, because I'd never been interviewed like that before and I really wanted to be accepted. I loved the creative process and was eager to get started on the next phase of my life. But by the time the acceptance letter came two months later, I'd upended my own plans to step out of the spotlight and found myself at the center of a full-scale media storm. And I can tell you that no one from CNN wanted to interview me about my inspiring mood boards.

Around the same time back in December that I was working on my mood boards for the fashion school application, a friend introduced me to Nick Mulholland, a public relations guy at one of the biggest PR companies in the UK, to get advice on whether to make some sort of public statement about being gay or to just let the word seep out organically over time. I met with Nick at his office and told him everything about my story and explained that I wasn't sure what I wanted to do. He suggested that I do some writing, just put my thoughts down on paper and think about the kinds of questions I'd likely get from the media and how I might answer them.

So I took Nick's advice and a few days later sat down at my computer and created a file called "LetterOfLife," and wrote straight through without stopping to change anything. I wrote the letter mostly for myself because it helped me get some things off my chest that I wanted to share with people who might have known me but had no idea what I'd been struggling with. Here's what I wrote:

The Next Chapter . . .

Things are never what they seem . . . My whole life I have felt different, different from my peers, even different from my family. In today's society being different makes you brave. To overcome your fears you must be strong and have faith in your purpose.

For the past 25 years I have been afraid, afraid to show whom I really was because of fear. Fear that judgment and rejection would hold me back from my dreams and aspirations. Fear that my loved ones would be farthest from me if they knew my secret. Fear that my secret would get in the way of my dreams.

Dreams of going to a World Cup, dreams of The Olympics, dreams of making my family proud. What would life be without these dreams? Could I live a life without them?

Life is only complete when your loved ones know you. When they know your true feelings, when they know who and how you love. Life is simple when your secret is gone. Gone is the pain that lurks in the stomach at work, the pain from avoiding questions, and at last the pain from hiding such a deep secret.

Secrets can cause so much internal damage. People love to preach about honesty, how honesty is so plain and simple. Try explaining to your loved ones after 25 years you are gay. Try convincing yourself that your creator has the most wonderful purpose for you even though you were taught differently.

I always thought I could hide this secret. Football was my escape, my purpose, my identity. Football hid my secret, gave me more joy than I could have ever imagined . . . I will always be thankful for my career. I will remember Beijing, The MLS Cup, and most of all my teammates. I will never forget the friends I have made along the way and the friends that supported me once they knew my secret.

Now is my time to step away. It's time to discover myself away from football. It's 1 A.M. in London as I write this and I could not be happier with my decision. Life is so full of amazing things. I realized I could only truly enjoy my life once I was honest. Honesty is a bitch but makes life so simple and clear. My secret is gone, I am a free man, I can move on and live my life as my creator intended.

Before closing my computer I read through the letter once and remember thinking that if I ever did anything with it I'd better have my sister Katie read it first to fix the punctuation and grammar. She's the writer in our family. But for now I was content to let the letter sit on my desktop as I went about my life in London.

About two months later, on February 15, 2013, I was at home with Scott talking with him about whether I should come out and make a statement or not. A lot had changed in those two months, both for me personally and for gay people in general. And while my focus was very much on myself, my relationship with Scott, and living my newly liberated life, I was aware of the dramatic political and social shifts under way in attitudes toward gay people and marriage equality in the United States, the UK, and across the Western world.

In the United States, 2013 began with President Obama embracing marriage equality in both his inaugural address and State of the Union speech, which was extraordinary from a historical perspective, but to me it just seemed like the right thing to do. What felt so hopeful about the President's support and the other efforts I was hearing about was that the world was opening for people like me, even if the world of men's professional sports remained something of a throwback when it came to the inclusion of openly gay athletes.

The biggest change for me personally was that it had become clear to me by early February that Scott and I had different ideas about what our relationship was going to be. He wasn't someone who was all that expressive about his feelings, but after spending a few months getting to know each other and spending a lot of time together he wanted to know where I saw our relationship going, because he was ready for some kind of commitment. The problem for me was that I didn't share Scott's wish. I said, "Honestly, I don't know, I love spending time with you, and you're great, I'm attracted to you, but I've just come out and, besides, I'm going home for the summer." I think I surprised myself by how direct I was, because being direct about anything involving my emotions was something still so new for me.

Scott knew I was planning to return to London to go to school in September, but there were still so many question marks for me about my life. I explained to Scott that, having just come out, I wanted to explore being gay and wasn't nearly ready to settle down. I then said something that I've since learned is a total cliché, but was something I really felt in my heart. I said, "Even if we're not dating we need to be friends."

And very reasonably he responded, "It might be too hard for me." I said, "Well, let's try." So we did.

It was soon after our conversation that we were at the dinner table at my place talking about whether I should make some sort of statement. By that time I think Scott was growing bored with my back-and-forth, indecisive one-man debate. I asked him, "Do you think I should say something one day?" And he said, a bit impatiently, "Say it or don't, but whatever!" I'd never shown Scott the letter I'd written and saved on my desktop, so I showed it to him. He read it and got really emotional and said, "This is really good." I think, like anyone who is gay and had to struggle as they came to terms with their sexuality, he could relate to my struggle and it reminded him of what he'd lived through.

Scott said the letter was perfect, that he wouldn't change a word, and that I should post it. I thought he was messing with me, but he assured me that he wasn't. There was something about how he reacted, in combination with my wish to tell more people that I was gay and that I was finished with soccer, that gave me the confidence to press the button on my computer to post the letter to my blog. Then I went to my Twitter account (I had eighty thousand followers back then) and tweeted: "Getting some shit off my chest," and included a link to the letter.

I had two competing thoughts immediately after posting my letter. First, I thought, *Oh, shit, now everyone will know.* And almost simultaneously I felt, *Everyone will know and now I am free.* I had no way of knowing how people would react, but I figured it would be both positive and negative. But mostly it just felt so good to be out from under the "Big Lie." I felt light, like I could start fresh now that I'd shared what my struggle had been. I had nothing to hide anymore, so it was done. Right after I pressed "Enter" and posted the letter I turned off my phone, put away my laptop, and Scott and I went out for some drinks at Shoreditch House, a club in London.

In retrospect, this was another one of those moments when I chose not to think about the potential impact—on me or anyone else—of what I'd just done. Did it occur to me that I still wasn't out to my grandparents? Had I considered that people in the media might have a few questions for me and when they couldn't find me they'd be on my sister Alicia's doorstep first thing in the morning? Did I think to talk to my mom to give her a heads-up that I'd decided to make a public statement and she'd better call her parents if she wanted to get to them before the *New York Times* or ESPN did? No. None of it. But to be fair to myself, I also had no idea of the kind of media feeding frenzy I'd unleash by sharing publicly my deeply personal feelings about so much that I'd wanted to get off my chest for so long.

While we were having drinks, Scott couldn't resist checking Twitter and said that the reaction was crazy. Good, but crazy. I said I didn't want to look, so he put away his phone and we headed to Pizza East for some pizza.

It wasn't until the next day, after Scott and I had arrived in Brighton on the southern coast of England to run a half marathon, that I turned on my phone and immediately had a call from my mother. And she was mad! It hadn't occurred to me that because I went on radio silence reporters would understandably seek out those closest to me for their reactions, and the first two people they found were my mom and Alicia. Here's my mother's memory of what happened:

I had just come out of a meeting and I had all these messages on my phone from people in the media asking me to comment on Robbie's letter, which I'd never seen. The last I heard from Robbie he'd said he wasn't going to say anything to anybody. And now he'd sent out this incredible, heartfelt message to the entire world and we weren't told about it. I tried to reach Robbie, but his phone was off.

My first thought was that I had to get to my parents before CNN showed up at their door, because I didn't want them finding out from a stranger that Robbie was gay. So I canceled out my office day, grabbed a copy of the letter Robbie had sent to me when he first told me he was gay, and drove down to my parents. And the whole time my phone is ringing off the hook.

I finally get to their house and sit my parents down and say, "Mom, you're a mother. Dad, you're a father. I want to read you something my son sent me," and I read them Robbie's letter. We all cried. My mother said, "Are you kidding me? Do you think I care if Obbie Ogers is gay? He's my grandson. I love him."

I was so relieved by how my parents embraced Robbie without a moment's hesitation, but the whole thing felt like such a betrayal, like Robbie had thrown his family under the bus without thinking.

It wasn't just my mom who was angry. Alicia was furious with me. This is what she remembers:

Here I was, laid out in bed sick, and so sick that I've called in sick to work. I'm thirty pounds heavier than I

normally would be, just a pregnant wreck. And I get a
call from the hospital with a message that the *New York
Times* called and wants to speak with me. I guessed it
was about Robbie, but I had no idea what was going on.

Within minutes of that call there's a knock at the
door, and I get myself out of bed and answer it and there's
some random reporter staring at me. I closed the door on
him and locked it. I got my mother on the phone and she
told me what happened and I thought, *What a selfish
prick! I kept your secret. I'm here for you no matter what.
But then you expose me and our entire family without any
warning.*

When I calmed down and had the chance to think, it
occurred to me that maybe the reason Robbie didn't ask
me in advance what I thought was because he was worried I would talk him out of it, or worried that I'd say,
"Robbie, you said you didn't want to be the gay poster
boy," and maybe I would question him. Robbie can be
very stubborn and when he makes up his mind about
something, he needs to jump. But it was just so incredibly selfish, as if my life was not important.

My mother and sister were both right. What I did was incredibly selfish. But that didn't keep me from being defensive,
at least at first, because I felt they weren't being considerate of
me and what I'd been through for all those years. So when my
mother told me she was mad at me because I didn't warn her
and that she was getting questions from reporters who had the
impression from my letter that my family wasn't supportive of
me, I got mad right back. I said, "Well, Mom, actually it was

hard growing up and you guys aren't the most gay-friendly people I know of. And there's a reason I'm like this—that I'm so fearful, and that it took me so long to come out. So think about *me* for a second." Mom was silent for a moment and then said, "Okay, true." But while that was true, what the letter didn't reflect, because it was two months old, was that my family had really rallied around me in the weeks since I'd first written it. The next day, once I'd cooled off, I tweeted a note about how amazingly supportive my family had been and how much I loved them.

When Alicia got me on the phone she asked if I'd posted the letter as a "big fuck-you to everyone," which it wasn't, and I tried explaining. I said, "It didn't have anything to do with you. I wasn't thinking about you guys at all. And I'm sorry I wasn't, but I was so miserable and just wanted to be free to express myself."

What I failed to consider when I posted my letter was that in choosing to come out of the closet in such a public way, I outed my family. Just because I was ready to let everyone know I was gay didn't mean they were prepared for or welcomed the kind of public attention that followed. I was the public person. I was used to it from soccer, even if I'd never talked to the press about being gay. But now my family was in the spotlight for something that was still new to them and I hadn't even bothered to give them a heads-up or the chance for them to share their feelings with me about my decision. I could argue that I just didn't anticipate all the media interest, but I should have at least considered the possibility and warned the people closest to me.

I've had to accept that what I did—or at least the way I did it—was wrong, thoughtless, and totally selfish. I hope my mother and sister and the rest of my family all know how sorry I am for thinking only of myself and for putting them in the position of having to fend off the press because I wanted to go public but didn't feel ready to face the media's questions myself.

Scott was right that the reaction to my letter was crazy. I got thousands of emails and calls, and the media people were contacting Leeds, Stevenage, the Columbus Crew, and my family, but no one from the press managed to find me. Not that anyone needed a comment from me to report the news that I'd come out. Very quickly the story was everywhere, and virtually all the news reports were positive and supportive. Within days of my coming out people would recognize me on the street or in coffee shops and say, "Congratulations!" and ask me questions.

In the days after posting my letter, I had some breathing room to absorb what had happened and to begin reading through some of the tweets and messages. I heard from former teammates, friends, and thousands of complete strangers; from children struggling with all kinds of secrets and parents struggling to accept their gay children; from gay people trapped in heterosexual marriages and straight supporters who felt compelled to reach out to me because my story touched them or inspired them in some way.

I remember being so shocked by one email I received from a married gay man. He said, "I'm gay and married to a woman and expect I will always be. No one but you knows that I'm gay. I've attached a photo of my wife and me with our three children. I admire your courage." I received a lot of those kinds of notes and it made me realize that I was hardly the only gay person who had lived such a lonely and isolated life.

Virtually all of the notes I received were supportive, and I even had one from a Catholic priest that was the complete opposite of what I might have expected. The subject line read: "So sorry that the Catholic Church wouldn't support you during your youth." He went on to write: "As a Catholic priest significantly older than you are, I'd like to state how saddened I was to read about your years growing up in the Church and getting such a negative message from it about yourself when what you need to hear from the Church was just the opposite. You need to hear how much the God who created you loved you and cherished you beyond your wildest dreams."

That email was breathtaking. Coming from a Catholic priest, that meant a lot to me, although by this time I no longer considered myself Catholic because the Catholic Church was uncompromising in its anti-gay views. So how could I be a part of a Church that thought I was defective? What I had come to believe was that I was gay because God created me this way and that he had a reason for making me this way. I remember thinking, *Okay, this is going to be hard and a lot of people won't believe you were created this way, but this is not a weird thing, it's simply who I am. My Church may not accept it, but I do, so it's time to move on.* I still consider myself a Christian and have a strong faith in God, and while I'm happy that the new Pope has said comparatively accepting things about gay people, I still don't see a place for myself in the Catholic Church.

I was totally astonished by how many people I heard from and the range of people who contacted me. In fact it was so overwhelming that I ignored a lot of what came in and often didn't respond to emails and tweets. But I remember hearing from CNN anchor Anderson Cooper and Gavin Newsom (the former mayor of San Francisco, who is famous for issuing marriage licenses to same-sex couples before it was legal to do so in California); and Andy Cohen from the Bravo network tweeted a supportive note, too.

I also got tweets and emails from all kinds of gay rights organizations and I heard from Rufus Gifford, who is gay and served as President Obama's finance director on his campaign and has since been named U.S. ambassador to Denmark. The funny thing is I was so out of the loop on gay stuff that I didn't know who a lot of the people were who wrote to me.

One note that had a big impact on me came from my national coach, Bob Bradley. He wrote to me and said, "I'm so proud of you. To step out and do this, to be strong enough to make a statement and show who you are to the world, that's amazing." I really didn't expect that from him because he's older and very traditional, although I never heard anything homophobic from him. I also heard from his son, Michael, who played on the national team with me, and he said, "I've known you for a long time and respect what you did." I'd lived with him in Florida when I played on the U-17 national team and had heard him say homophobic things, so I didn't know how he would react. Getting that supportive note from him was a surprise and it meant a lot to me.

I also heard from Sigi Schmid, my old coach from the Columbus Crew, who texted me and said, "Don't retire from playing because you came out. If you want to play, you should play. You'll be accepted." Sigi's new team, the Seattle Sounders, posted a short video on YouTube in which four of the guys on the team, along with Sigi, talked about their support, and their teammates' support, for me and my decision to come out. It was really incredible.

The outpouring of support from the world of professional soccer was beyond anything I could have expected. There were encouraging messages from lots of my former teammates, including some from my former Leeds United teammates. Darren Bailey, the director of football governance and regulation for the Football Association in the UK, told the *Columbus Dispatch* newspaper: "Whether Robbie stays in the game or steps away for a break he has our full backing." The *Dispatch* also published a statement from the Chicago Fire's head coach, Frank Klopas, who said, "Yesterday I thought he was a very good player and I still think that today. Should Robbie want to return to the game, we would still be open to him being part of the Fire." Longtime U.S. goalkeeper Kasey Keller said what I was hearing from more than a few U.S. soccer players: "The bravery of Robbie Rogers is commendable, I hope he realizes that he doesn't need to retire. He will be more supported than he knows."

U.S. Soccer, the official governing body Major League Soccer, couldn't fit everything into one tweet, so here are the three they sent out:

U.S. Soccer @ussoccer Statement on @RobbieRogers: "As a
Federation we support all our athletes who have had the
courage to address this deeply personal topic."

U.S. Soccer @ussoccer statement contd: "We are proud of
Robbie. He has been an outstanding representative of our
National Team program for many years."

U.S. Soccer @ussoccer ". . . We support him and wish him great
success in the future."

In addition, my old team the Columbus Crew put out a statement: "Robbie Rogers was a valuable member of the Columbus
Crew and a dedicated community ambassador during his time
with the club. The organization wishes him every success in
his future pursuits."

A couple of old teammates, Colin Clark and Marc Burch,
who'd recently gotten in trouble for using homophobic slurs
(both were suspended for three games), sent out supportive
tweets. Marc wrote, "So much love and respect for my fellow
Terp and friend @robbierogers hope to see you on the pitch
again soon!" Colin wrote, "The courage @robbierogers has
shown coming out is of the class most men can only dream of.
I was lucky to call him a teammate. I hope his bravery helps
pave a path for others to know they don't need to hide." Like
I've said before, lots of people who reflexively use anti-gay language aren't really anti-gay.

One of the best texts came from my dad, who wrote, "I'm
proud of you. When you came out, you scored the ultimate
goal." He later told me that I was the bravest person he knew.
You can imagine how good it felt to hear that, especially given

what painful memories I have of my dad yelling at me for not being the kind of boy he expected me to be.

Reading through lots of the emails and tweets and listening to the messages and watching the video clips from just after I came out publicly, it almost feels like I'm reading all the nice things they say about someone after they're dead. But fortunately I'm still here to be reminded how wrong I was about what the reaction to me would be if I ever told the truth about my life. The whole experience has been beyond humbling and heartening.

It's funny. You would think that with all the notes and messages and phone calls that came in I wouldn't notice the one that I *didn't* get. But there is one coach who had been an important mentor, who helped guide me throughout my career, and who I thought I'd hear from but didn't. He helped advise me when I was first considering going to residency in Florida when I was in high school, and later I had the good fortune to play for him on several occasions. It really saddened me that even after I wrote to him twice he was silent. I can't help but wonder why. I guess everyone has their own issues.

Even after coming out publicly, I was still thinking I'd fade away into a normal life. But that clearly wasn't happening, and with so many requests for interviews I started thinking that I couldn't continue with the silent routine. I was even offered £30,000 in the UK to give a newspaper interview, but money wasn't the issue for me. It was about me being comfortable and feeling ready to talk to a reporter about my story, so I said no to the money.

Part of the problem for me was that I didn't trust anyone and feared that the media would try to spin my story to suit their needs. Whenever reporters write anything about anyone, I'm always worried about how it will be changed. Maybe they'll use a quote out of context, or maybe they just won't understand, maybe I didn't articulate it well. But I felt like I didn't have a choice. So with advice and help from my agent and some of my magazine friends I chose to do interviews with the *New York Times* and the *Guardian*, which is based in London. Before the actual interviews, I asked to talk first with the reporters off the record so I could get a sense of them and they could get to know me a bit and see that I didn't have any agenda other than to talk about my experiences. Also, I hoped that if they got to know me a bit, it would be harder for them to write a negative story, at least that's what I hoped.

In advance of the interviews, my agent's PR company wanted to prep me, and I argued with my agent because I didn't want someone telling me what to say. But my agent insisted, and after asking me three questions the PR people realized that I could answer the questions on my own. I was a little nervous about the whole thing, but I went into it knowing that I was just speaking for myself. I speak from the heart. I think about what I'm going to say and I say it. I'm not worried about holding back and I don't have anything to lie about. Not anymore. So I figured there was nothing they could ask me that could catch me off guard.

At the *Guardian* I met with a few different reporters who had reached out to me and decided to work with Don McRae, who is a beautiful writer. One of the first things he told me was that his daughter had read my letter and that she started crying. We sat for two hours and talked. Don and I also did a Google Hangout session, so people could watch it online. It was perfect.

After the two articles were published simultaneously on March 29, 2013, the response was really positive. Tons of emails came in with messages like: "Thanks for representing the gay community with class."

It is funny when someone says, "Representing the gay community . . ." or says, "Thanks for giving gay soccer players a voice." I can't take any credit for playing either role because I don't represent the gay community and I'm not giving anyone a voice other than myself. If anything, I like to think that I'm speaking for myself and for all people who feel like they've been discriminated against. That's a role I'm happy to embrace.

CHAPTER 13

NOW WHAT?

With the two big newspaper interviews behind me, I really thought that I was done. I'd said everything I wanted to say, answered all the questions I was asked, and now I could quietly go back to being a regular person. Well, get to be a regular person for the first time. My plan was to head home for a visit, stay a couple of months, return to London, and then start fashion school. A new beginning. But things didn't turn out as I'd expected and I didn't go back to London. Instead, I found a very public and incredibly rewarding life at home in California, one with real purpose that I'd never thought was possible when I spent all those years hiding. But I'm getting way ahead of myself. First, I had to get home, and even that turned out to be anything but a private moment.

The first stop on my trip from London to Los Angeles was New York City. Arnaldo Anaya-Lucca, the head photographer for Ralph Lauren, the clothing company, had asked me to come by to meet with the Ralph Lauren team. They were thinking of using me for one of their advertising campaigns. So I arranged to stay with a friend who had an apartment on the Upper East Side of Manhattan, right by Central Park. It couldn't have been a more perfect location because I could take my new dog on long walks and explore the park together. I'd always wanted a dog and loved Scott's dog, Dougal, who was a dachshund/miniature poodle mix. Coincidentally, one of Dougal's brothers was still available, so I adopted him and named him Jeffrey.

Up until this point in my life I'd never stopped to take a real break for myself and just chill. When you're a serious athlete with the goal of playing professional sports you never take a breather. You're taught to go, go, go. If you take a break you'll lose your edge—and your momentum. So from the moment I first started kicking a soccer ball on the sidelines at my sisters' games until I retired from professional soccer, I'd never stopped playing, training, competing, and pushing myself toward the next level. Now all that was behind me and for the most part it was fun and it was great to live without constant pressure. If I wanted to go for a walk in Central Park with Jeffrey instead of working out, I went for a walk.

The meeting at Ralph Lauren's flagship offices on Madison Avenue was exciting because I love Arnaldo's photography and thought it would be great to work with him. But it was also totally embarrassing. You sit in a room and everyone looks you over like you're a lamb chop and gives you compliments. For example, one woman said, "You're *so* beautiful!" To try to get the focus off me because it made me so uncomfortable, I said,

"Here's my dog"—I had Jeffrey with me—"isn't he cute?" That just seemed to make things worse. I haven't heard from them since the meeting, but maybe there'll be an opportunity to work together in the future.

While I was in New York, my agent asked me if I would go on *Anderson Cooper 360* on CNN, and he also told me that ABC's *Nightline* was interested in doing a story and wanted to fly home with me to California and record me seeing my family for the first time since telling them I was gay. Without really thinking about it, I said yes to both.

With the Anderson Cooper interview, I wasn't at all nervous until I walked onto the set. Not because it was my first live television interview since coming out, which it was, or because it was Anderson Cooper—I knew he was gay and also figured there wasn't anything he could ask that I couldn't answer. It was the bright lights. I felt like I'd walked into an interrogation room. But it went well. Anderson was really nice and asked about why I came out, what it felt like to hide my real self from everyone, including my family, and what it was like to hear my friends in the locker room say derogatory things about gay people; and I talked about what it was like to grow up without any gay role models in professional sports.

Anderson also asked if I felt pressure to play soccer again because people were urging me to go back. I surprised myself by saying that I still loved soccer and that there was a good chance I might come back to it, although it wasn't something I was seriously thinking about at that point beyond maybe doing some training with the LA Galaxy. I explained that I really needed a few months to hang out with my family, surf, and just relax before I did anything. What I didn't say was that soon after I came out publicly, Bruce Arena, the coach for the LA Galaxy, had sent me a message that if I wanted to come to a game or a training I should feel welcome. He said, "Robbie, we've known you for a while, and we know you're a good person, and we'd love for you to train if you ever want to." So going back to training was already something I was thinking about. Now that I didn't *have* to play and didn't have to worry about hiding the real Robbie Rogers, I started to miss it.

So I answered all of Anderson's questions one at a time without breaking a sweat, and then he said, "Yeah, when I came out when I was in fifth grade . . ." and *I* thought, *Does everyone even know you're gay?* Even though I knew he was gay, I didn't know he was out; that's how clueless I was.

Before I gave the final go-ahead to *Nightline*, I had to check with my mom to be sure it was okay to have another camera crew with me when I got home. I was in the early stages of working with my friend Steve Nash on a documentary about my life, so there was already going to be a camera crew waiting at the house when I walked in the door. And my mom was cool with that because she thought it could be helpful to other families to see how I'd been embraced after coming out. Like I expected, she said it was fine for *Nightline* to be there, too.

I was so excited on the flight to L.A. I was already excited just to be back in the United States after a year away. And now I was going home to see my family and they were going to see me as me, not someone I was pretending to be. For the first time I wasn't going to have to be on guard. I wouldn't have to censor myself, which meant I could really listen to what they were saying without always trying to anticipate a question they might ask that I'd have to duck or answer with a lie. So as I looked out the window of the plane, with the lights of L.A. spreading out to the horizon and Jeffrey sleeping at my feet, I thought about what it would be like to be with my family. And instead of getting that tight feeling in my stomach that I'd always gotten in the past when I was going home to visit, I had an overwhelming sense of lightness and clarity. For the first time in as long as I could remember, I had nothing to hide.

Our flight wound up being very late, so it was just my mom and my sister Katie who were waiting up for me when I got home at midnight. I know I had a big smile on my face as I walked through the door. Katie came running down the hall and hugged me and she was crying. Then my mom hugged me, too. Mom was more emotional than usual, but it's always emotional with us when we haven't seen each other in a long time. They both had such big smiles.

My mom was great on *Nightline*. If you'd told me a few months before that my mom would be comfortable being interviewed for a national television news program about her gay son, I never would have believed it. But there she was in the kitchen standing next to me saying these really supportive things. She said, "It was a time of sadness . . . to think that there was something my son suffered with by himself. And then it was a great moment of joy to think we were all together, that we could share it, and that we could start something new." And I said, "Exactly true." And it was.

The next day, when the whole family was home for dinner, and I was sitting around the table with my mom and my brother and sisters and we were laughing and joking and having a good time, I was thinking, *This is what it should be like when you're sitting with your family.* I'd waited for so long for this moment, to be comfortable with myself, for them to know who I really was, and for them to still love me—and maybe even love me more because I wasn't hiding. They could see that I wasn't any different from the son and brother they had always known, but happier, because I was finally free to be myself.

I wasn't home for long. A few days after landing at LAX, I was back on a plane, this time heading for Portland, Oregon, to be a panelist for an event that would leave me thinking that I wouldn't be going back to school in London after all. Nike and GLSEN were cosponsoring the Nike Be True LGBT Youth Forum for high schools kids from across the Pacific Northwest who were active in their schools' GSAs. I'd had a long relationship with Nike because they'd sponsored me since I was sixteen, so it made sense that they'd reach out and invite me to be a panelist. But until then I'd never heard of GLSEN or GSAs. Once I came out it was like getting a crash course in being gay. I'd been so deeply closeted that I really knew nothing about gay history, the gay civil rights movement, or organizations like GLSEN. Fortunately, I'm a quick study, especially if I'm interested.

GLSEN stands for Gay, Lesbian and Straight Education Network. It's a national organization dedicated to "ensuring safe schools for all students." What I learned at the Nike forum is that eight out of ten LGBT students are harassed at school because of who they are. And GLSEN's mission is for "every student, in every school, to be valued and treated with respect, regardless of their sexual orientation, gender identity or gender expression." It would have made such a huge difference for me if I'd gone to schools that lived by those values.

GSAs, or gay-straight alliance clubs, are school-based organizations at thousands of high schools and middle schools across the country, where LGBT kids and their straight allies can go to support each other and work on fighting discrimination, harassment, and violence in schools.

I was one of six people on the panel, which included a transgender man who cofounded TransActive; a lesbian who worked at Nike; the founder of the Trevor Project; the leader of PFLAG Portland Black Chapter; and Alex Horsey, a young man who founded and runs an organization called Project Believe in Me, which is a youth-led organization dedicated to ending bullying. The Trevor Project provides crisis intervention and suicide prevention for LGBT youth. PFLAG is an organization with chapters across the United States and around the world for parents, families, friends, and allies of LGBT people that's dedicated to "moving equality forward." And TransActive is "focused on serving the diverse needs of transgender and gender non-confirming children, youth, their families, and allies."

We did two sessions, each lasting an hour, with a total of about five hundred students. At first I was nervous because I'd never done anything like that before and didn't know what to expect. When we got to the auditorium, I stood off to the side with the other panelists and watched as the kids came in and talked to each other with a sense of excitement. You could tell these kids were a bit different and I could feel their positive energy. For one thing, they seemed so confident and comfortable with themselves. And a lot of them dressed in an edgy way, had dyed hair, or had crazy haircuts and more expressive makeup, not like you'd see in Rolling Hills Estates where I grew up.

The moderator, Tim Hershey, an executive from Nike, introduced us one by one and the kids all applauded as we came up on stage. Tim started off by asking us a half dozen questions. He asked us to give advice to young LGBT high school students based on our own experiences. When it was my turn to respond, I said, "It's tough for me to give any advice because I didn't come out until a few months ago, but from my experience I'd suggest finding someone you can talk to away from your friends and family. Someone you can trust, who will be supportive and keep your secret if you're not ready to share it with anyone." I wish I'd had even one person to talk to when I was young so I didn't have to feel totally isolated.

When it was time for the students to ask questions and make comments, I was really impressed to hear about what they were doing at their particular schools to educate people and fight homophobia: "This is what we're doing at our school . . ." "We're the first GSA to have this or that program . . ." "We won the right to bring our boyfriends and girlfriends to the prom . . ." Their mind frame was so different from mine when I was growing up. If I ever saw something on television about gay men and women fighting for equality, I'd turn away or shut it out because I was so closeted. To hear these students talk so confidently and optimistically about what they were doing was inspiring. From their comments I could tell they really believed that they could make things better, and by the time the two sessions were over I was convinced they would, and that maybe I could, too.

One of the students who came up to the microphone to ask a question started out by saying, "This was the best day of my life!" It felt like he was speaking for me, because it turned out to be one of the best and most transformative days of my life, too. These brave students made me realize what a coward I was by comparison. I was never a part of any of these clubs when I was in high school. I never spoke out when people were treated badly, whatever the reason. But here they were, already out at fourteen, fifteen, sixteen years old, fighting *against* discrimination and *for* equal rights and respect for everyone, when all I'd done was come out and share my story. And it wasn't like I came out because I was trying to help anyone. I was just trying to save myself by getting out from under all the lies.

The first thing that occurred to me after attending the forum was that Nike could do these events all across the country, videotape them, and put it all up on YouTube so young people around the world could watch and be inspired by their peers and the panelists. I could see how much these kids got out of the experience, meeting other students who were doing the same thing, drawing strength from each other, and making new friends. I said to my agent, "Nike should do twenty or thirty of these a year," and while it turns out they weren't interested, that didn't mean I couldn't do something on my own. I thought, *I'm twenty-five. I have this public platform. I've had such a positive response. I can't just go back to London and go to fashion school, not when I have the chance to help young gay people feel better about themselves than I did at their age and to help the LGBT civil rights effort move forward.* God had given me this opportunity and I felt an obligation to embrace it, because it felt like the right thing to do.

That's when I decided to go back to playing professional soccer. I had the chance to use that platform to help people, and if any of these kids had been in my position that's what they would have done. Even without much of a platform they were willing to organize, speak to school administrators, and go into regular classes to talk about their experiences and educate people. As an out professional soccer player, I could do my part by setting an example and being a role model for that young Robbie Rogers who was just starting out in his sport and wondering whether he could be himself and still do what he loved. And even for kids who weren't interested in sports, if they saw me doing what I wanted to do as an out and proud gay man, then maybe they would feel that they could be themselves and do the things they dreamed of doing. I could be an example of someone whose difference not only didn't get in the way, but also made his life better.

These amazing kids at the Nike forum—in combination with the hundreds of young people who wrote to tell me that I'd inspired them to come out to their parents or given them the inspiration to stay alive—inspired me to test myself, to see if I had the courage to go back in the locker room and onto the field as an openly gay man. After Portland, I decided it was time to find out if I did.

CHAPTER 14

BACK IN THE GAME

It was one thing to challenge myself by saying that I was getting back in the game. It was another to actually do it. Before I called my agent to tell him what he'd wanted to hear since I first told him I was quitting—he'd been calling me once a week since December urging me to go back to playing—I needed to test myself both physically and emotionally to be sure I was strong enough and brave enough to do it.

I knew I could train with the LA Galaxy if I wanted, but before I got in touch with Bruce Arena, the Galaxy's coach, to take him up on his offer, I wanted to sound out one of my friends, Landon Donovan, who played for the Galaxy, to see what he thought the reaction would be from his teammates. The truth was that despite how inspired I'd been by the kids at the Nike forum to step forward and be brave, I was terrified at the prospect of walking back into the locker room as an openly gay man.

What if they ostracized me? That fear had kept me in the closet for years. And if they *did* ostracize me I couldn't imagine returning to professional soccer. I knew I didn't have the emotional strength to do that.

Landon's been with the LA Galaxy for years. He used to be the captain. He's a national team player, probably the best American player ever. I met him when I was really young and we've played with and against each other, including on the national team. And I knew he didn't have an issue with me being gay; he'd taken a very public role appearing in public service announcements for Major League Soccer's "Don't Cross the Line" anti-discrimination campaign.

I sent Landon an email in which I said, "As someone who knows the locker room, what do you think it will be like? I'm a little afraid." He wrote right back and said, "Let's get a coffee and talk about it." We met at Landon's place in Manhattan Beach, and took his dogs to a nearby park for a walk. I told him I was afraid to be in a locker room with a bunch of straight guys, that it was an environment that had really hurt me in the past. I said, "I'm afraid that if I walk into the locker room the guys will be awkward and silent around me or just very careful about what they say, like they were walking on eggshells." I was more fearful of the potential awkwardness and silence than I was of anyone saying anything bad to me directly. "I don't want to be treated differently," I said. Landon said, "It might be weird for the first few days, but then they'll get over it. We've got a great group of guys, but this is something we've never experienced before, so you'll need to give them some time."

Talking to Landon helped, and although I was still anxious, I wanted to see what would happen. Maybe I'd walk in and be like, *Okay, this was an awful experience, I'm never going back*. Or maybe it wouldn't be so bad. Whatever the outcome, I felt compelled to at least give it a shot, so I sent Bruce Arena a message and said, "I'd love to come in and train, just to see if I can do it."

The morning of my first practice I woke up early and had breakfast. I was staying with my mom in Huntington Beach, so it was only a thirty-minute drive to the training center in Carson. I got there around eight-thirty and walked downstairs to the training room and lockers, which are all underneath the stadium. I was really nervous and scared about what the initial reaction would be like, but it wasn't nearly as awful as the feeling I'd had in my stomach during all those years when I was hiding. I knew the whole coaching staff and the medical guys, because I'd been there before when I was recovering from my broken ankle. People said, "Hey, Robbie, how are you?" "Hi, Robbie, nice to see you." Everywhere I went in public at that point, people would say, "Congratulations!" or "Thank you!" so I was expecting to hear a little of that, but at the stadium no one said a word about what I'd done. I was more surprised than disappointed.

Then I walked into the locker room. I think anytime you go into a locker room as a player who's not signed it's a bit awkward. I think some guys didn't know what to say to me, but a lot of the guys didn't know me that well, so it was hard to say whether they were awkward because I was gay or awkward because they didn't know me, or both. But whatever it was, it wasn't bad. So I changed and headed out onto the field where I'd played as a kid and where I played with the Columbus Crew when we won the MLS Cup. It couldn't have been more familiar ground, but everything was different now.

The real surprise was how out of shape I was. It had been

five months since I was on a field, and it showed. We did some ball work and passing, and we played with big goals but a smaller field. I was tripping over my own legs, like Bambi. I wasn't sharp and got winded easily, but I was really happy to be out there playing. Whatever awkwardness there might have been in the locker room disappeared once we were on the field. I had a great time and was proud of myself for doing it.

I decided to go back for training the next day and the day after that. I wanted to see if I continued to get better and continued to enjoy it, and as long as I felt comfortable, I decided I'd keep going back. So for the next few weeks I trained four or five days out of every seven. It was very normal, casual training, and it got easier, and I started talking to guys about the usual things you talk about.

The one time anything gay came up was when one of my teammates, Todd Dunivant, who had the locker next to mine, called me up to ask if I'd heard that Jason Collins, the NBA player, had just come out. He was good friends with Jason, so as soon as he heard about Jason's cover story in *Sports Illustrated* he called me. I'd just read about it on Twitter and started getting calls from the media asking me for a statement, as if I were an expert on gay athletes. What I said to everyone was, "I'm just as surprised as you guys, and I'm happy for him, but I don't know Jason."

I spoke to Jason that day; he got my number from Todd. The first thing I said after he introduced himself was, "Congratulations, but it feels a little weird to congratulate you for being honest." Jason had called to ask how I dealt with my PR, and I told him, "I retired, and I wasn't with a team, and that was the biggest reason I did it, because I wanted to do it on my terms." I knew that if I'd stayed with soccer my team would have controlled who I talked to and when, and I knew I didn't want to talk to anyone, because I wasn't ready. I said to Jason that I thought it was going to be more difficult for him because he was still with the NBA, even though he wasn't signed to a team. I said, "They're probably going to ask you to do all kinds of interviews, but you might want to take some time for yourself."

I met Jason for breakfast a month after that. He's a nice guy, friendly and funny. I really like him. You can tell if someone has the right motives, and the impression I got when I met Jason was that he was like me. He came out because he wanted to be happy and free. I remember saying to him, "I hope you play, because there's a lot of education that will go on in the locker room." The NBA is so much bigger in the United States than soccer and reaches into all parts of the country, and basketball players are icons in their communities, so his playing as an out gay basketball player would have a bigger impact on those people than my coming out. (Jason wound up not being picked up by a team for the 2013–2014 season, but was signed by the Brooklyn Nets in February 2014, and finally made basketball history with his NBA debut as the first openly gay NBA player on February 23, 2014.)

By the time I met with Jason I'd already decided to go back to playing professional soccer and my contract was in the works. I naïvely thought it was going to be an easy process because I already I knew I wasn't going to play anywhere but in Los Angeles near my family, so that meant the LA Galaxy or Chivas, the other team in L.A. That's what I told my agent about two weeks after I'd started practicing with the Galaxy.

I'd also talked to my mom to see what she thought. I told her that I'd been having a good time and thought I could go back to playing and helping people and enjoying it. She said, "I knew you were going to go back. That would be amazing." I said, "I'm only going to do it if I can play here in L.A., so you guys can come and I can have that support system, because what if things don't go that well?" She agreed and said, "That's probably the smart thing to do." My mom knew all too well what had happened in the past when I took a big step far from home, from my family and friends, and she watched as I crashed and burned. I'm sure she didn't want that to happen again. I also talked to my dad and to my sister Alicia, and they agreed with my mom and said essentially, "We know soccer has made you happy for a long time, but only do it if it'd make you happy and if you're comfortable doing it."

So I called my agent and asked him to sound out the Galaxy to see if they were interested in having me sign on. And they were, but there was a hitch. The Chicago Fire Soccer Club owned my rights, which meant they had to agree to trade me to the LA Galaxy. For reasons that really don't make sense to me, when I left the United States for Leeds the Columbus Crew still retained my ownership rights. That's just how it works in Major League Soccer. While I was gone, Columbus traded my rights to Chicago. And it turned out that the Chicago Fire didn't want to let me go without getting something in return—money or players. When my agent told me this, I said, "Look, tell them I'm going back mostly to help people, to set an example, and they're being rats about this." I'm sure my agent didn't use that exact language when he went back to them, but whatever he said, they wouldn't budge. So I asked to meet with the owners, who live here in Los Angeles.

At the meeting I said, "I'm not going back to playing if I have to move to Chicago. I'm only going back if I can play in L.A. I've had an amazing year, but it's also been a rough year and I need to be near my family and friends for support." I went on to explain that I really wanted to go back to help people, to make a difference, that by returning to professional soccer my example would have a positive impact on young gay athletes who wanted to play professional sports and, for that matter, on all gay people who had felt like outcasts. "If they see that I can go back and play the sport I've always loved," I said, "then they'll see that they can do what they love, too, without being afraid that being gay will hold you back." The owners told me they understood, that they'd make it easy. But they didn't.

What happened next went on behind the scenes, so I only learned about it after the deal was done. Mike Magee—who is an amazing athlete who had done a lot as a player for the Galaxy—was from Chicago, had a new baby girl, and wanted to be near his family. So when he heard about the possibility of a trade involving me, he asked to be the one who was traded. Given that Mike is such a great player, the Galaxy never would have traded me for Mike if he hadn't asked, so I have a lot to thank him for. We both got to go home.

While the deal was still being worked out I continued to train with the Galaxy and on May 12 celebrated my twenty-sixth birthday, which was a birthday celebration unlike any I'd ever had in the past. I invited some of my gay friends and some of my former high school classmates, who were straight, to join me for dinner at a restaurant and then we all went out to the Abbey, which is a West Hollywood gay bar and restaurant. For my straight friends it was their first time at a gay bar. I thought they might feel a bit awkward, but they all loved it, and danced and had a great time. It was something new to them and afterward they said they wanted to go back.

I was amazed! If you'd told me just a year before that this was how I'd be spending my birthday I never would have believed that my straight high school classmates would be supportive of me—let alone accept me—that they'd have no problem hanging out with my gay friends, that they'd enjoy going along with all of us to a gay bar, that they'd dance with us, and that they would want to go back. I'm gay, they're not, but all that mattered to them was to be there for me, and I found that very moving. And even though years before when I'd been their friend in high school I'd heard homophobic stuff come out of their mouths—which made me feel terrible about myself—I came away from that celebration knowing that my straight friends were fundamentally good guys.

Twelve days after my birthday celebration I signed with the Galaxy. Once the announcement went out, I was interviewed by a lot of reporters and asked what it felt like to be going back to professional soccer. What I said to *USA Today* sums up best what was on my mind. I said, "I want to compete on the field. I want to make it back to the national team. I want to be a role model. I have a lot of motivating factors working for me right now. There's a lot to be excited about. It's awesome to be part of a movement that is changing our society."

I figured it would be a few weeks before I played in my first game—I still had a long way to go in my training—but on the day I signed, Bruce Arena told me, "We might play you this weekend against the Seattle Sounders." All I could think was *Okay, here we go!* I wasn't fit or sharp or anything, but I was excited about the possibility of playing again. Nervous, too. It was all new. A new team. A new stadium (the StubHub in Los Angeles). New fans. And a new uniform, too. They asked me what number I wanted and I chose 14, which was the number I'd worn in training. Johan Cruyff, a really good Dutch player I admired when I was younger, and who played the same position as I did, wore number 14, so that was perfect.

The Sounders game was set for Sunday, May 26, and driving over to the stadium that evening I was really scared. Not the scary feeling I'd always had about the possibility of someone finding out I was gay. This time I was scared because I wanted to represent myself and my team and my family well and was worried that people would criticize me if I played poorly. And I felt the additional pressure of representing gay athletes and the larger gay community. I was also nervous about how the fans would react. And there was always the possibility that I'd never get off the bench and that made me nervous, too. So to take my mind off everything, I called Alicia and we talked about Jeffrey. It helped.

Getting ready in the locker room wasn't really different from when I was training with the team, but now we were getting ready for a game and I had to remind myself that some of the nervousness I was feeling in the pit of my stomach was just left over from when I was still hiding. Something I've discovered is that just because you're not hiding anymore doesn't mean those old feelings of fear just evaporate. I'd been hiding for so long and scared for so long that the bad feelings were automatic. I was going to have to train myself to be normal and not always on guard that someone was going to say something that hurt, or fearful that I'd get drawn into a conversation where I had to lie or sidestep a question.

The twenty-seven-thousand-seat stadium was filled nearly to capacity with about twenty-five thousand fans, including my whole family: my mom and dad, my grandparents, Alicia, Coco, Timmy, Katie, some of their partners, and some of my friends. Before the game Sigi Schmid, my old coach from the Columbus Crew, who was now the Seattle Sounders' coach, walked over to our bench to say hello. He gave me a really warm hug and said, "Good to have you back." Marc Burch, who was now a Sounders substitute, along with a few other former teammates and friends, also came over to say hello and wish me luck.

There are always several photographers and reporters at games, so it was nothing out of the ordinary that a few of them were taking my picture, and there were a handful of reporters who wanted to ask me questions, including a guy from ESPN, who asked what my dream scenario would be for how the game might play out. I said that it would be perfect if we were up 4–0 and I came in for the last ten or fifteen minutes of the game. And that's exactly what happened.

With thirteen minutes left in the game we were up 4–0, and I was called in to replace midfielder Juninho. As I ran out onto the field to play professional soccer for the first time as a whole person, whatever nervousness I'd been feeling disappeared. I could hear the crowd cheer and could feel the huge ear-to-ear smile on my face. Apparently there were fans chanting my last name, and although I couldn't hear it myself, it was an incredible adrenaline rush to soak up the roar of the crowd. It was one of the happiest moments of my life, especially knowing that my family was there to share it with me and were cheering along with everyone else for the real Robbie Rogers.

It was really great how so many of the guys made me feel welcome. As soon as I ran onto the field for warm-ups I got hugs from a couple of my old teammates, Brad Evans and Marcus Hahnemann, who both were playing for Seattle. Brad and I had been roommates when we played for the Columbus Crew, and Marcus and I both had been on the national team.

And when I stepped onto the field to play I couldn't have felt more at ease or more normal—more normal than I'd ever felt before. Then it was just a matter of doing what I'd always done in the past, which was playing my part on the field. I felt like I did fine. I touched the ball a few times, made a tackle, and completed some passes. It was an easy game for me because we were up 4–0, we had the ball, and Seattle wasn't playing that well.

The best thing of all that day was having my family in the stands and knowing that they were there for *me* and not someone I pretended to be. That made me happier than when I won the MLS Cup. Whether or not I scored, whether we won or lost, I was just happy to be able to share that experience with them.

After the game there was a press conference with maybe a

couple dozen media people. If I had to recall what I said in the moment I couldn't tell you because it was all a blur, but what I said to Billy Witz at the *New York Times* is what I remember feeling: "It was really perfect. We won, which is most important. My family was here, my friends. My grandparents. I've kind of been on this huge journey trying to figure out my life. And now I'm back here. I think kind of where I'm supposed to be."

After the game I took an ice bath to keep my knee from swelling up, took a shower, and went home. I had training the next day, so I couldn't go out with my family to celebrate, although I called them when I got home. Everyone congratulated me and said it was great to have me back. It was great to *be* back!

That night, when I got into bed, I said my prayers and thanked God for giving me the courage to go back to playing professional soccer. For what felt like the first time in my life, I was really at the place in life where I felt like I was meant to be.

I woke up on May 27, 2013, to news headlines about my "historic" return to soccer and, just like when I first came out in my blog post a few months before, messages flooded in from friends, old teammates, and coaches, as well as politicians and celebrities congratulating me on being the "first openly gay man to play in one of North America's top five men's professional sports." One of my favorites came from Ellen DeGeneres, who tweeted: "I'm proud of Robbie Rogers and his team, the LA Galaxy. What an incredible weekend for acceptance, for sports, and equality."

I'm no expert on the history of gay people in sports, but I knew there were a lot of openly gay and lesbian athletes who were "firsts" before me and were firsts in much more difficult times. I owe a debt of gratitude to people like Justin Fashanu, Billie Jean King, Greg Louganis, and all the other brave gay and lesbian athletes who had the courage to step forward before me. Some, like NFL player Dave Kopay, who came out in the mid-1970s, were already retired when they announced they were gay. Others, like tennis star Martina Navratilova, came out while they were still actively engaged in their careers.

And, to be honest, I could easily argue that I'm not even the first openly gay man to play in one of the top five men's professional sports in North America. Glenn Burke, who played baseball for both the Los Angeles Dodgers and the Oakland A's from 1976 to 1979, was up front about being gay with just about everyone he knew and even talked to reporters about it. But back in those days sports journalists didn't write about homosexuality, period. Burke died of AIDS-related causes in 1995, and I first read about him last year in an article by Allen Barra that was published in the *Atlantic*.

Whatever my place in history, on the morning of May 27 there was no disputing that I was the only openly gay man playing in one of the top five men's professional sports in North America. (I know there are some sportswriters who don't think Major League Soccer should be included along with football, basketball, baseball, and hockey, but I think they're wrong and so do millions of soccer fans.) And because of my status as a "first" and/or "only," I've had lots of opportunities to make a difference by speaking publicly about my experiences. Having a public platform also inspired me to launch an anti-discrimination campaign—called BEYOND "it"—that goes beyond labels and stereotypes to celebrate what makes us unique. The point of the campaign, which I developed with a group of really talented straight guys, is to embrace difference in a way that makes us stronger instead of driving us apart.

I'd like to leave you with just three examples of memorable experiences I've had in the past year that were important lessons for me. The first forced me to recognize that I still have a lot to learn about living an open life. The second taught me that no matter who you are and where you live, being gay still makes you a potential target for other people's hatred. And the third experience reminded me to be optimistic, because there's every reason to hope that before long no young LGBT athletes dreaming of a pro career will have to live in secrecy as I did just so they can play the sports they love.

The first experience that proved to be an important lesson was one I walked into without thinking. And that was the problem.

I've surprised myself by how comfortable I've been sharing my story in the media, with my teammates, with friends, and even with my family. What's been a lot harder is sharing what I think of as my "personal life"—the things straight people routinely talk about, like dating and relationships, but are exactly the things I instinctively *don't* talk about. It's not even that I think about hiding that information. It's that it doesn't occur to me to share it, to be open with my family in normal ways. The secrecy is automatic, and coming out publicly didn't change that instinctive reflex. If I'm really honest with myself, a lot of this is about shame—shame that I'm something I've long thought of as sinful, inferior, and a personal defect.

In this case, the thing I chose not to tell my mother—that didn't *occur* to me to tell my mother—was that the friend who was joining us for dinner one evening in October 2013 was in fact my boyfriend. And we were having dinner at *his* house. First, some background. I had met Greg at a party on Pride Day in June and we started dating soon after. I never said a word to my mother about Greg even though from early on I knew that it wasn't a casual relationship.

Then in October my mother told me that she hadn't been seeing enough of me since I'd returned from London. She was right. I'd invited my mom to various events I was involved in, but those weren't the kinds of places where we could actually talk. So I said, "Okay, fine, Mom. How about next Tuesday night? And why don't you bring Alicia and baby Lily [my new niece] and Jeffrey?" Jeffrey spends most of his time at Alicia's house these days because I've been traveling so much, and consequently he's become the shared family dog. I'll let my mom pick the story up from there:

> When we got to Robbie's place he said, "We're going to have dinner at a friend's house. But let's go get some coffee first and go for a walk." After the walk we get in the car and go to his friend's house. He introduces us to Greg, who I can tell almost immediately is this wonderful person who wears his soul on his shoulders. But very quickly I sensed that Greg was not just a friend, although I wasn't quite sure who he was to Robbie. *This is familiar*, I thought to myself. *The way Robbie and Greg interact with each other is familiar.*

At some point early in the evening, when I still wasn't quite getting it, Greg caught me a little off-guard when he said, "I want to tell you, I think it's really wonderful how you've embraced Robbie, how you've accepted this." And I said, "I love my son. What mother wouldn't?" Greg responded, "Not everyone has had that experience." So I'm listening and watching and thinking and then I realize, *Wait a minute. He's not just a friend. He knows something about me. He's talked to Robbie about me. Why would that be?* And then it hit me.

I didn't say anything during the course of the evening but I was thinking, had Robbie been heterosexual and had a wonderful woman come into his life, he would have said, "I've met this wonderful woman, I've been dating her, this is what I love about her . . ." But with Greg, he hadn't said a word to me and left me to figure it out on my own.

When I got home that night I called Robbie and said, "My whole life, since you were born, I would pray that someday you would bring home someone wonderful, someone I would love, who I thought would love you and take care of you and make you a better person. And I think I just met that person. Is Greg someone special in your life?"

Now, that's the moment when I should have come clean with my mother and apologized, but I'd really convinced myself that I hadn't done anything wrong. I'd already told Alicia about Greg and thought she'd told Mom. And even if she hadn't, I just assumed Mom would figure it out once she met him, which she did. But clearly that's not the way you want to introduce your mother to your boyfriend for the first time.

At first I didn't know how to respond to my mom's question, but I quickly came up with an answer: "Well, yes, we're seeing each other." My mom didn't let on that she didn't like my answer, because when I asked her later about what she felt in the moment, she said she was thinking, *Oh, my gosh, that's way too sterile a response for what I'm asking you. Please don't rob this from me by hiding Greg from me, because this is one of my prayers being answered.* What she actually said instead was "Why didn't you tell me?" And I said, "I'm so sorry. I just assumed Alicia had told you." But it should have come from me.

Since that first dinner together I've worked hard at not making assumptions and not hiding my relationship with Greg. I never thought it would be so challenging to be normal, but it's getting easier as I get more practice, so much so that when Greg came home to Huntington Beach for our family Thanksgiving, he fit in so comfortably that it didn't even feel strange to me that it was all so normal. It just felt right.

The second experience I had, the one that gave me firsthand experience of what it feels like to be threatened simply because you're gay, happened in West Hollywood, the very gay-friendly neighborhood where I live.

Greg and I had just left a club at the Standard Hotel on Sunset Boulevard. We hadn't stayed long, so it was maybe eleven-thirty p.m. We crossed over to the north side of Sunset and walked east with the hope of finding a cab. Then right by the Andaz Hotel this white Jeep, with the windows down, drove by slowly in heavy traffic going in the opposite direction. I glanced over and saw there were four young guys in the Jeep, maybe late twenties, all with short, spiked hair. Then I heard one of them say in a loud enough voice for me to hear, "Fags!" Instantaneously I tensed up, because the way he said "fags," with so much hate in his voice made it feel like a threatening situation. I turned to Greg and asked, "Did he say that?" And Greg said, as astonished as I was, "He did!"

In that moment I wanted to walk up to the Jeep and say, "Get out of your car and say that to my face." Getting called "fag" made me angry and my first instinct was to confront the guy. But then I thought, *That would be stupid. There are four of them and two of us. You never know. He might have a gun, he might be looking for a fight.* I had the feeling that if I even looked at them they'd be out of their car and kicking the shit out of us, so I said to Greg, "Let's just ignore them and keep walking."

Given that West Hollywood is where gay people come to live to be free of all this stuff, I was really surprised to have this happen. And it made me wonder what makes people want to do that, to use language they know is hurtful, to threaten someone by calling him a fag. Was that guy just trying to act macho with his friends to show how straight he was? Was he looking for a fight? Was he bored? Did he have some reason to hate gay people, or at least dislike them enough to yell, "Fags!" at two total strangers he thought were gay?

I'd heard that this sort of thing happened all the time, even in West Hollywood. But until you experience it yourself it's easy to think, *Oh, that was a long time ago,* or, *It's so rare and random it would never happen to me.* But it did. People think times have changed with the younger generation, but there are still a lot of homophobic people everywhere.

In the past, that sort of thing drove me deeper into the closet, but now it just motivates me more, to be myself, to talk about my experiences, to continue doing what I'm doing. And because I have the love and support of my family, I know I can face whatever comes my way.

The final experience I wanted to tell you about came a month later and it was the total opposite of that evening with Greg in West Hollywood. I was in Europe promoting the launch of my BEYOND "it" anti-discrimination campaign and was invited to attend a professional soccer match in Ghent, Belgium, to help launch their national campaign against homophobia in Belgian soccer.

If my flight from New York hadn't been delayed by weather, I would have seen for myself that the outside of the stadium in Ghent, the Ghelamco Arena, was lit up in rainbow-colored lights—the rainbow flag is a symbol of gay pride around the world. And because I wasn't able to be there in person they showed a video on the huge stadium screen featuring me talking about my experience of coming out. They pulled out key phrases as I spoke and superimposed them over the video, like, "Coming Out Was the Best Thing I Ever Did," "Finally I Could Be Fully Myself," "Being Yourself Means Being a Better Player," and "So Let's End Homophobia in Football." Just a year ago, in my wildest dreams I never could have believed I'd be up there on that screen delivering *that* message to thousands of soccer fans. And I missed all of it!

The next day, when I finally got to Belgium, I arrived in time to be interviewed on a national television talk show, which was where they showed me what I'd missed. I was interviewed along with my old friend and teammate Sacha Kljesten, who plays in Belgium for the Anderlecht football club. Sacha and I had been friends since I was twelve and he was fourteen. We've played together on the national team and at the Olympics. When I first came out, Sacha sent out this really supportive tweet. He wrote: "100% love and support for one of my best friends Robbie Rogers. You will be missed on the pitch. Amazing talent. Amazing person."

Even though I was totally exhausted and jet-lagged by the time I took my seat on the set next to Sacha, it was thrilling to see both the images of the stadium's exterior in rainbow colors and the video of me delivering the anti-homophobia message. It made me feel so good—that I'd come out, spoken out, and that I now had the opportunity to get behind a national campaign in Belgium to help make things better for gay people in soccer and sports in general. Feels like I came out at just the right time to be a part of a movement around the world to end homophobia in professional sports. At least that's my hope.

This past year has been an extraordinary and surprising journey for me. If you had told me two years ago that I would come out, play soccer as an openly gay man, and share my experiences with the world, I would have said you were insane. The new life I've found since coming out—which is a lot different from the one I'd expected to have out of the public spotlight—has been an amazing ride, with some great highs, some real disappointments, and plenty of frustrations, particularly on the soccer field, where yet more injuries have often kept me on the sidelines.

The biggest and best surprise of all was discovering how blessed I am to have such a loving family and strong group of friends, all of whom have had my back every step of the way. God's path for all of us is so unpredictable, but I've come to believe that if you keep a level head and your eyes wide-open, your own special path will become clear to you.

I still feel like I have my whole life ahead of me, and for as many years as I have, I intend to keep pushing for equality in whatever ways I can. Many women and men aren't lucky enough to have the kind of support that I've had both in coming out and returning to soccer. Nonetheless, it is my sincere hope that my story has reminded anyone who is different in a way that leaves them feeling isolated—as if no one in the world could possibly know how they feel—that they are truly not alone.

To be continued . . .